Pastoral Development Planning

Julian Prior

Development Guidelines No. 9

Oxfam
UK and Ireland

First published by Oxfam (UK and Ireland) in 1994

This edition transferred to print on demand in 2008

© Oxfam GB 1994

ISBN 978-0-85598-204-1

A catalogue record for this publication is available from the British Library.

All rights reserved. Reproduction, copy, transmission, or translation of any part of this publication may be made only under the following conditions:

- with the prior written permission of the publisher; or
- with a licence from the Copyright Licensing Agency Ltd., 90 Tottenham Court Road, London W1P 9HE, UK, or from another national licensing agency; or
- for quotation in a review of the work; or
- under the terms set out below.

This publication is copyright, but may be reproduced by any method without fee for teaching purposes, but not for resale. Formal permission is required for all such uses, but normally will be granted immediately. For copying in any other circumstances, or for re-use in other publications, or for translation or adaptation, prior written permission must be obtained from the publisher, and a fee may be payable.

The information in this publication is correct at the time of going to press.

Available from:

BEBC Distribution, PO Box 1496, Parkstone, Dorset, BH12 3YD, UK
tel: +44 (0)1202 712933; fax: +44 (0)1202 712930; email: oxfam@bebc.co.uk

USA: Stylus Publishing LLC, PO Box 605, Herndon, VA 20172-0605, USA
tel: +1 (0)703 661 1581; fax: +1 (0)703 661 1547; email: styluspub@aol.com

For details of local agents and representatives in other countries, consult our website: www.oxfam.org.uk/publications
or contact Oxfam Publishing, Oxfam House, John Smith Drive, Cowley, Oxford, OX4 2JY, UK
tel +44 (0) 1865 472255; fax (0) 1865 472393; email: publish@oxfam.org.uk

Our website contains a fully searchable database of all our titles, and facilities for secure on-line ordering.

Published by Oxfam GB, Oxfam House, John Smith Drive, Cowley, Oxford, OX4 2JY, UK

Oxfam is a registered charity in England and Wales (no 202918) and Scotland (SCO 039042). Oxfam GB is a member of Oxfam International.

Front cover: Pastoralists and their camels in Merka region, southern Somalia.
Andrew Njoroge/Oxfam

Contents

Lists of figures and tables   iv

Preface   v

Acknowledgements   vii

1 Introduction   1

2 The forces of change: redefining the problem of pastoral development   6

3 A critical review of the history of pastoral development projects   23

4 Case study: the Erigavo Erosion Control and Range Management Project   56

5 The development approach of the Erigavo Project   71

6 Rangeland management and the Erigavo Project   97

7 Identifying an appropriate model for pastoral development   109

8 Conclusions: changing policy directions   120

Notes   130

References   133

Index   144

List of figures

2.1 The cycle of rangeland degradation and famine: an episodic and iterative process   18
2.2 The forces of change and suggested causal linkages within the pastoral sector   21
4.1 Erigavo District, Sanaag Region, North-West Somalia/Somaliland: towns and private range area   57
4.2 Problem definitions and causal linkages operating within the Erigavo District   69
5.1 Schematic representation of the 'learning process' approach adopted by the Erigavo Project, and its relationship with data-collection, intervention-design, and implementation   77
5.2 Participatory development as an evolutionary process   89
7.1 The 'autonomous replicate' model of development   113
8.1 Predisposing factors and triggers of famine in vulnerable populations   123

List of tables

2.1 Estimate population growth–rates for six selected countries with significant pastoral populations   11
3.1 Twelve commonly recurring factors contributing to the failure of pastoral development projects   24

Preface

This book is intended for community-development planners with a professional interest in pastoral development. It is particularly directed at those whose experience of pastoral development is limited and who require an understanding of where pastoral development has been, and where it may be going in the future.

Historically, pastoral development in the South has been the province of technicians, particularly those with training in range science. Recently, however, those with broader development concerns, especially from the non-governmental organisations (NGOs), have turned their attention to pastoral development. Often these people are deeply concerned with the economic, social and political rights of pastoral peoples. They may have extensive skills in development planning, but lack the necessary technical skills of pastoral development. For these people the practical techniques of pastoral development often seem to be shrouded in mystery. This book is an attempt to demystify pastoral development through an examination of the impacts of the more common forms of project experience. However, the discussion is less concerned with the technologies themselves than it is with the development environments and the development processes into which the technologies are often inserted. The book also suggests future goals for pastoral development to which development planners may be able to contribute.

Community-development planners potentially have much to contribute in this area. To date, pastoral development has done little to lessen the vulnerability of pastoral communities to disasters such as drought and famine. Nor has development contributed substantially to strengthening the economic, social, and political rights of pastoralists. Indeed, despite development efforts over the last 40 years, there is considerable evidence to suggest that the security of African pastoralists is diminishing, while their vulnerability to disasters such as famine is increasing.

The book can be divided into three sections. The first, which includes Chapters 1, 2, and 3, examines the recent forces of change within the pastoral sector and appraises the development record in the light of the needs of pastoral peoples. The second section, Chapters 4, 5, and 6, examines in detail the experience and lessons of one pastoral development project: the Erigavo Erosion Control and Range Management Project funded by Oxfam (UK and Ireland) in North-West Somalia (an area which has since declared itself 'the Republic of Somaliland'). The third section, Chapters 7 and 8, speculates upon the future of pastoral development. Chapter 7 examines approaches to pastoral development suggested by the preceding discussion. Chapter 8 highlights a number of high-priority future directions for pastoral development policy.

Acknowledgements

I wish to thank a number of people who contributed in various ways to this book. Clare Oxby, Richard Moorehead, and John Rowley made valuable editorial comments on early draftrs of the full text. Roy Behnke made suggestions on an early draft of Chapter 3. Clare Oxby contributed material dealing with restocking and paraveterinary projects. Catherine Robinson's skilful editing transformed my original draft.

My thanks go to Oxfam (UK and Ireland) for giving me the opportunity to work in a development environment where the human needs of a pastoral people were allowed to shape the nature of the development process.

I am grateful to the pastoralists of the Erigavo District of North-West Somalia/Somaliland who happily shared their culture with me during the many hours we spent together.

I thank my wife Suleikha, now an unusual cultural mix of Somali-Australian, who offered me her observations, her views, and her support throughout.

Final responsibility for the opinions expressed within this book of course rests entirely with the author.

Pastoral Development Planning

1

Introduction

The history of pastoral development projects in Africa has largely been an inventory of failures. In *Does Aid Work?*, a review of multilateral and bilateral agencies' development experience published in 1982, Robert Cassen found that the African pastoral sector experienced the greatest concentration of failed development projects in the world. The highest proportion of project failures was attributed to sub-Saharan countries.

The primary goals of pastoral development projects usually include the arrest of environmental decline, or improvements in animal productivity, or both. Yet despite considerable expenditure on research and development programmes within the African pastoral sector over the last 40 years, environmental degradation continues unabated, and pastoralist communities are more prone than ever to poverty, and more susceptible to drought. The development literature has been citing the shortcomings of pastoral development projects and programmes for some years. Yet the same mistakes appear to be repeated with each subsequent project, moving one reviewer (Goldschmidt 1981: 117) to comment that he wondered why writing was ever invented!

In general the poor record of pastoral development can be attributed to two interdependent causes. The first relates to weaknesses in pastoral development policy. Until recently pastoral development policy has been almost completely absent from the development planning process. Even when policy has been articulated, the policy debate has been narrowly focused, and preoccupied with technological and macro-economic issues. Consequently pastoral development policy has often failed to reflect the needs of pastoral peoples.

The second and related cause of the poor record of pastoral development concerns the shortcomings inherent in the nature of the development projects most often attempted. Some of these shortcomings reflect the policy vacuum in which development has operated. Others are concerned with the nature of the project-development process adopted, or the technologies attempted.

The book's objectives

This book aims to help answer the question of why the history of pastoral development projects has been so unimpressive. It seeks to suggest ways in which to improve this record. The book has five objectives:

- To explore the recent and rapid changes which are confronting pastoral peoples.
- To identify the reasons for the recurring shortcomings in pastoral development projects, and to attempt to explain their persistence.
- To suggest ways to overcome these shortcomings.
- To describe the successes and failures of one pastoral development project in the Erigavo District of North-West Somalia/Somaliland.
- To explore future directions for pastoral development policy; to seek new definitions of the pastoral development 'problem'; and in doing so to define outcomes of pastoral development which may be termed 'desirable'.

The pastoral environment

Pastoralists can be defined as those who primarily derive their living from the management of livestock (sheep, goats, cattle, and camels) on rangelands. Rangelands are those areas where limitations such as climate (rainfall and temperature) or topography restrict the use of land to extensive grazing of natural pastures, rather than cultivated pastures or fodder crops.

Pastoralists may be *sedentary*, more or less permanently settled with their animals within a defined area; they may be solely *nomadic*, moving with their animals and transportable homes over irregular routes, seeking pasture and water for their animals almost continuously; or they may practise *semi-nomadism* or *transhumance*,

Introduction

Somalia: a camel loaded with sticks, mats, twine, and skins — the components of an aqal, the traditional nomadic tent

whereby they move with their animals over more or less regular routes, settling for part of the year in a permanent home area.

The sedentary pastoralist represents the Western pastoralist model, such as found in the United States and Australia. The African model, if there is one, would be more closely represented by the nomadic or semi-nomadic pastoralist. Of those people in the world defined as pastoralists, more than half are in Africa, 15 per cent are in America, and fewer than one per cent in Australia (Sandford 1983: 2).

Pastoralists may derive all their income from grazing livestock, or a portion of income may be derived from agriculture. Those who engage in both pastoralism and agriculture are termed *agro-pastoralists*. In dry areas, owing to extremely variable rainfall regimes, agricultural work is an opportunistic, high-risk undertaking. Agro-pastoralists in these areas commonly view their agricultural production as a supplement to their livestock-raising activities, rather than *vice versa*.

The term 'pastoral environment' as used throughout this book implies much more than the physical environment. The pastoral environment will encompass the pastoralists (both male and female), their grazing animals, and the physical, economic, social, and political contexts in which they live. The pastoral environment is one of immense complexity. Individual pastoralists, when making management decisions with regard to their grazing animals, will be influenced by a wide variety of factors.

First among these decision-influencing factors is climate, particularly rainfall, and its variability over time and space within the arid and semi-arid rangelands. The distribution and timing of rainfall determines where, when, and how much pasture and water will be available to the grazing animal. This in turn will influence, along with other factors, the pastoralists' decision to move with their animals.

Pastoralists are influenced in their decision making and the identification of their goals and needs by other factors also:

- economic considerations (both monetary and non-monetary)
- social concerns
- political factors
- legal constraints or incentives
- ecosystem variables (other than climate).

Pastoralists thus operate in a pluralistic and complex planning environment influenced by a number of factors, some or all of which may be in a state of rapid change. Pastoralism is a dynamic system. Efforts at pastoral development, to be successful, must recognise and understand the dynamics of the system into which they plan to intervene.

The meaning of 'development' depends upon who is doing the developing and who is receiving the benefits of the development. Large multilateral donor agencies may employ an entirely different definition of development from small non-governmental organisations (NGOs), even though both types of agency may be working in the same area, attempting to solve the same problem. The various organisational definitions of development are discussed later in this book. For the moment we can use Sandford's (1983: 4) generalised definition of development, which states that it is the 'conscious pursuit of certain objectives with a view to increasing welfare'.

Over the past 40 years or so, a number of pastoral development projects employing a variety of Western-trained 'experts' have entered the pastoral environment, all attempting to solve the pastoralists' 'problem' — however that may be defined. Among the ranks of these experts have been the physical or rangeland scientists (botanists, range ecologists, soil scientists, range extensionists, foresters, animal scientists, etc.) and social scientists (anthropologists, sociologists, geographers, and economists). Yet despite the huge investment in financial and human resources over this period, the history of pastoral development projects in Africa has largely been one of failure. Projects have failed to address effectively issues such as environmental degradation, pastoralist poverty, and the vulnerability of pastoral communities to ever-recurring droughts.

This book's first objective is to examine how we might define the pastoral development problem. We will do this by looking at the evidence for a number of new and powerful forces of change confronting pastoral peoples. To a large extent these forces of change are beyond the control of pastoral communities. Yet these changes have very much defined the nature of pastoralists' current and future development needs.

2

The forces of change: redefining the problem of pastoral development

Introduction

The factors which determine growth or decline within the pastoral sector have undergone rapid change over the past 50 years. While accurate measurement of these changes is not currently possible, we can study the evidence which supports the nature and direction of the changes. The factors at work may be summarised as follows:

- increases in pastoral populations
- changes in the densities of pastoral populations
- increased spontaneous settlement of formerly nomadic or semi-nomadic pastoralists
- a trend towards market-oriented livestock production
- increased land degradation.

Pastoral population increases

Population growth-rates within pastoral societies have become an increasingly fundamental issue in the field of pastoral development. The importance of population growth lies in its implicit links to land degradation and pastoral communities' susceptibility to famine. The supposition that pastoral populations are increasing at rapid rates is often used to suggest that the net ecological carrying capacity of the range has been exceeded, resulting in the gradual destitution of

The forces of change: redefining the problem of pastoral development

pastoral people. Yet there is little hard evidence to support the belief that pastoral population growth-rates have substantially increased in recent times — except in instances where formerly nomadic pastoralists have settled.

In any discussion of the population demography of pastoralists, several difficulties immediately arise. The first is the paucity and poor quality of data, explained by the isolation and mobility of pastoral populations. There are very few longitudinal studies of individual populations over extended periods of time.

The literature suggests that many human populations in Africa have undergone a period of rapid growth since the start of the colonial era. Broad regional studies such as those conducted by the World Bank (1992) and the UN (1982) have supported this view. However, there is considerable disagreement over extrapolating to particular pastoral populations from these observable whole-country trends. Nor can we make valid extrapolations to pastoral communities from empirical population studies of urban or agricultural communities.

There is evidence[1] to suggest that pastoral populations in general exhibit lower population growth-rates than either urban or agricultural populations. There is also evidence[2] to suggest that population growth-rates increase among pastoral groups as such groups sedentarise. The theoretical mechanisms for changes in population growth-rates within non-industrialised countries of the South are still a matter for academic debate. Broadly this debate involves those who support evolutionary 'demographic transition' theories versus those who give weight to 'proximate indicators' (socio-economic changes) as causal factors of population changes.[3]

In brief, the transitionists argue that before the colonial period, African populations had high birth rates and high death rates. With the advent of colonialism and better medical care, they argue, mortality rates markedly decreased, while birth rates remained high, with the result that populations grew rapidly. Others have argued that the empirical evidence supports the influence of socio-economic change upon population growth-rates. In particular, average age at first marriage, level of education, and factors influencing the exposure of couples to the risk of conception are major determinants of fertility levels. Thus ideas about demographic causality remain speculative. In the absence of empirical data, judgements about rates of pastoral population increases must remain similarly speculative.

However, speculations regarding the link between rangeland

degradation and presumed pastoral population increases continue within the literature. The rangeland degradation currently concerning international observers and pastoralists alike is relatively recent, much having occurred within the last hundred years. For example, much of the range degradation of northern Somalia/Somaliland has occurred since the turn of the century.[4] Evidence from the Erigavo District (Prior 1992a) suggests that within that area significant degradation has occurred in the last 30 years. If, as suggested by some observers,[5] the net ecological carrying capacity of the range is exceeded in many areas because of pastoral population increases, several alternative explanations are possible:

• It may be that pastoral population growth-rates have not dramatically increased during this century, but have more or less maintained their previous historical levels. The fact that range degradation is now observed suggests that it is merely coincidental that some ecological threshold was exceeded during a relatively short space of time, over quite a wide range of environments and cultures.

• Perhaps as a result of some as yet unexplained influence, pastoral population growth-rates have increased dramatically during this century, up to a level where the carrying capacities of the range were exceeded.

• A third possible explanation is that we should not be concerned with population growth-rates *per se*, but rather with changes in the *density* of pastoral populations.

The validity of the first assertion is impossible to judge with any certainty. The pre-colonial population growth-rates of pastoral communities are unknown. In any event it is probable that they fluctuated widely over time, following environmental disasters, war, and outbreaks of disease. However, it is highly unlikely that a number of pastoral cultures, over a variety of environments, in maintaining their pre-colonial growth-rates just happened to reach numbers which exceeded the ability of the land to support them, all more or less at the same time.

Within the literature the second assertion is perhaps the most widely-proffered explanation for the occurrence of range degradation. Yet again, there is little circumstantial or empirical evidence to suggest that the rates of pastoral population growth have increased during the twentieth century. There is empirical evidence of increases in some urban and agricultural population growth-rates.

The forces of change: redefining the problem of pastoral development

It is probable that the isolation of many pastoral populations limited the impacts of modern medicine on growth-rates. For many of the pastoral tribes of Ethiopia and Somalia, for example, it is unlikely that mortality rates were significantly reduced through improved medical care. In such cases the 'demographic transition' argument would appear to have little relevance for explaining changes in the rates of population increase.

There is little doubt, nevertheless, that international famine-relief interventions have saved the lives of many thousands of pastoralists, particularly since the 1970s. However, one of the criticisms of international relief operations in dry pastoral areas is that displaced pastoralists who enter refugee camps and feeding centres tend to remain there permanently. Deprived of their livestock, they have no way of re-entering their industry, and consequently become dependent on continuing handouts of food. For example, combinations of war and drought during the 1970s and 1980s have resulted in almost a million displaced pastoralists now living permanently in refugee camps in Ethiopia and Somalia. Some of the Ethiopian refugees now in Somali refugee camps have been there since 1973.

The alternative argument is that population increases are due primarily to variations in the immediate determinants of fertility. This hypothesis suggests that fertility rates may increase in response to external socio-economic changes. Two socio-economic changes are reported over a wide range of pastoral populations. These are the spontaneous settlement of some pastoral communities, and the increased shift away from subsistence-based livestock production towards market-oriented enterprises. As we saw above, there is strong empirical evidence to suggest that settled communities exhibit higher population growth-rates than more mobile communities. Thus within those pastoral communities who settle, an increase in population growth-rates would be expected. As we shall see later, there is a tendency for increasing numbers of formerly mobile pastoral communities to settle. Thus there is at least circumstantial evidence that population growth-rates among pastoralists in areas of settlement may be increasing, though this is a relatively recent occurrence.

However, when we focus on the possible causes of land-degradation, perhaps more important than the rate of pastoral population growth is the issue of changes in pastoral population density.

Pastoral population densities

The concept of population density has two dimensions: that of the number of people, discussed above, and that of the area of land to which they are confined. As suggested, pastoral populations are probably increasing, but (except for instances where formerly mobile pastoralists have settled) there is little empirical or circumstantial evidence to suggest any change in the rate of increase. In any discussion of pastoral populations, land degradation, and drought susceptibility, ultimately the parameter which begs measurement is that of pastoral population density. Yet to quantify this parameter for any given pastoral community, one must be able to measure *both* the human population and the area of land available to them. Clearly this exercise would pose immense difficulties.

Nevertheless, as land is a finite resource, we can deduce with some certainty, for reasons given below, that the area available for pastoral uses is declining. If it is assumed that pastoral populations are increasing, ignoring the argument regarding changes to the rate of increase, there is strong circumstantial evidence for reasonably rapid increases in pastoral population densities during this century.

The pool of land available to pastoralists has diminished in favour of other competing land uses. Foremost among the competing uses has been agriculture, both dryland and irrigated; but in some areas, such as Tanzania and Kenya, large formerly pastoral areas have been lost to game-park tourism. Several authors[6] refer to the loss of land to agriculture from pastoralism. The effect of this loss of land to the pastoral economy is substantial, because it is usually the better-quality grazing land (with the best soil, rainfall, and location) that is transferred into agricultural use.

If we accept that the growth of non-pastoral populations will have the effect of increasing pastoral population densities through competition for land, then estimates of whole-country population increases take on greater significance when we try to discern trends in pastoral population densities. Table 2.1 indicates the estimated population growth-rates of six countries which have significant pastoral populations.

The significance of these figures is that in all cases except Kenya, populations are expected to continue to increase to the turn of the century. Consequently the loss of land from pastoralism to other uses will also continue during this period.

The forces of change: redefining the problem of pastoral development

Gir Gir Group Ranch, Kenya, where pressure on grazing is intense since Samburu herders were excluded from their former rangeland, now designated as the Samburu and Isiolo Wildlife Parks.

Table 2.1: Estimated population growth-rates for six selected countries with significant pastoral populations

	Average annual growth of population (per cent)		
	1965-79	1980-90	1991-2000
Ethiopia	2.7	3.1	3.4
Mali	2.1	2.5	3.0
Somalia	2.9	3.1	3.1
Kenya	3.6	3.8	3.5
Sudan	3.0	2.7	2.8
Mauritania	2.4	2.4	2.8

(Source: adapted from World Bank 1992: 268)

Another significant factor is that pastoralists have become less mobile over recent years, owing to the demarcation of political boundaries and the advent of regional conflicts. So even if animal and human populations had remained static during the post-independence period, their effective density would still have increased.

In summary, the evidence for increases in pastoral population densities is strong. Increases in some pastoral populations, increases in non-pastoral populations, losses of pastoral land to other uses, and the decreased mobility of pastoral communities are all contributing factors.

The sedentarisation of pastoral communities

The spontaneous (as opposed to government-induced) settlement of formerly mobile pastoralists has occurred within a growing number of pastoral communities. The settlement of nomads may be partial, entailing a change from a completely nomadic existence to a form of semi-nomadism, or it may involve a more or less permanent settlement. In settling, pastoralists may remain entirely animal producers, or move towards opportunistic agro-pastoralism, or they may give up their dependence on livestock completely and become agriculturalists.

Nomadic settlement and the privatisation of formerly public range have produced enormous changes in some traditional pastoral systems. From this writer's observations in North-West Somalia/Somaliland, settlement seems to be the result of a number of factors, some of which must act in concert to bring about this change. These factors can be summarised as:

- physical advantages of the area of settlement, such as better-quality, accessible pasture, and proximity to markets;
- increased density of livestock watering points;
- increased human population densities in some range areas;
- increased commercialisation of livestock production among some groups within pastoral communities;
- the emergence of a class of pastoral entrepreneurs, some of whom may not be pastoralists themselves, but who are willing to invest in livestock production by employing others.

The environmental prerequisites for settlement are that there should be a relative abundance of pasture and stock water for those

The forces of change: redefining the problems of pastoral development

maintaining livestock systems; or sufficient and reliable rainfall and productive soils for those undertaking agricultural production. For these reasons pastoralist settlement is more likely to occur in climatically favoured range areas. In terms of risk-spreading, agro-pastoralism has certain advantages in dry areas over either livestock production or agriculture alone. However, motivations for the movement of some pastoral communities towards more settled agro-pastoralism are more complex than merely being a reflection of a desire to spread environmental risk.

Several writers[7] have described dramatic changes in the political economy of pastoralism. Briefly these changes fall into four areas: the increased commercialisation of livestock production; a distinct economic and political stratification among formerly 'egalitarian' communities; an increased tendency towards pastoralist settlement and range enclosure; and, in some instances, an observable breakdown in the traditional systems of social organisation and co-operation.

Given that some or all of these processes have been observed in countries as geographically diverse as Somalia, Kenya, Sudan, and Niger, several questions arise:

- Are there simple causal linkages between each of these processes, or are there additional external factors bringing them into being independently?

- Are these changes desirable or undesirable in terms of the productivity of pastoral production systems; the social and economic rights of pastoral communities; pastoralist resilience to adverse climatic conditions; and the processes of land degradation?

In both Sudan and Somalia, Roy Behnke (1986, 1988) concluded that the effects of range enclosure on livestock and range productivity would be the following:

- a disruption in livestock production from the regional nomadic herd, possibly causing a decline in regional production;
- an alteration in individuals' access to grazing resources, causing an increase in the social and economic stratification of pastoral communities;
- increased rates of soil erosion and vegetation loss through over-cultivation and over-grazing.

Behnke noted that commercial systems of production associated with settlement had increased the supply of young high-quality male sheep for the Somali export market, and also that increases in mean farm size (including both agricultural and range lands) as a result of enclosure arose, not because of many individuals marginally increasing the size of their farms, but because of a small number of wealthy and politically powerful individuals greatly increasing the size of their holdings.

For many pastoral cultures, communal ownership of rangeland and the concomitant systems of social organisation are institutions which are hundreds or even thousands of years old. The magnitude of the changes to these institutions over the last 20 years is clearly immense. However, many of these factors are operating within other pastoral communities who have not responded by settling or by privatising public range.

Commercialisation of pastoral livestock production

Here we are concerned with the commercialisation of livestock production by pastoralists themselves. We are not concerned with efforts by external agents such as governments or development agencies to encourage or force pastoralists towards producing for the commercial market.

The transition from the subsistence production of livestock towards market-oriented production is a process that is difficult to define. Most pastoral groups conveniently described as subsistence producers will, for example, sell excess livestock such as young males and old females in the market place. What distinguishes subsistence groups from commercial groups is not so much the quantity of herd off-take for the market, but the quality of that off-take in response to the market demand. Subsistence producers aim to maximise subsistence production, i.e. meat and milk, for domestic consumption. Commercial producers sacrifice some of this subsistence production to increase the marketability of their livestock. Alternatively they can alter the composition of their herds, so that they are producing a type of animal which has a greater market value — for example, by shifting from goat to sheep production. Rather than conserving fodder to aid the survival of animals during the dry season or drought, a commercially oriented producer will conserve fodder to fatten animals for the market.

Clearly, however, there is a graded continuum between the predominantly subsistence producer typical of the African pastoralist and the completely commercial producer in the Western mould. In

The forces of change: redefining the problem of pastoral development

order to describe a pastoral group as progressing towards commercial livestock production, there must be evidence of behavioural changes over time which discount subsistence production in favour of commercial production.

Certain preconditions are necessary for the transition of a pastoral group towards commercial production of its livestock. Firstly, there must be strong market demand for a certain class of prime animal. Secondly, there must be the development of a cash economy within which can be purchased consumer items deemed desirable by the pastoralists. Thirdly, the pastoralist must decide that the other non-commercial needs or values attached to livestock (such as subsistence, or maintaining ties of kinship) have been either devalued relative to the commercial value, or satisfied, before the sale of 'excess' animals can take place. The satisfaction of the non-commercial needs is more likely to be achieved by a wealthy pastoralist with many animals than by a poorer pastoralist with few animals. Consequently owners of large herds have the ability to engage in and benefit from commercial livestock production and sale to a greater extent than owners of small herds. Some researchers[8] claim to have found evidence of these behavioural changes in Somalia, and other authors have identified similar processes in Kenya[9] and Senegal.[10] Swift (1976:454-5) suggests that potentially ...

> ... the most important changes are an increase in marketed animals of all species, a corresponding decline in the number of animals available for traditional loans and gifts of animals to those in need, a general loosening of traditional social and economic networks, and a reorientation of economic activity towards the market. This generally leads to a shift away from risk-avoiding strategies and a reduction in the ability of the pastoral economy to protect its members in times of crisis. Where these changes are accompanied by the formation of a modern state, the authority of which is simultaneously spreading in the pastoral areas, some of the political, social and economic functions of the pastoral society may also be shifted to the machinery of a central government.

It has been suggested[11] that the commercialisation of livestock production has had, and will continue to have, substantial impacts upon the role of pastoral labour. These impacts include displacement of labour from poorer households to commercialising households, a shift from payment-in-kind for labour towards wage labour, a decreased ratio of labour to livestock, and out-migration of labour from poorer households.

Clearly such fundamental changes in the social and economic fabric of pastoral societies, if realised, make adaptation immensely difficult for any pastoral community. Shifts away from group support, coupled with an increasing commercialisation of livestock production and social and economic stratification, may leave poorer pastoralists more and more marginalised. Poorer pastoral groups are less able to withstand and recover from periods of environmental stress such as droughts. When commercialisation is accompanied by settlement and the privatisation of formerly public range, it is the wealthier elite who claim disproportionately large areas of the best grazing and water access. To the detriment of poorer pastoralists, the elites maintain their hold over these areas through their more effective manipulation of the political system.

Land degradation

The issue of pastoral land degradation is one of intense debate. Many observers[12] believe that the process of irreversible land degradation, resulting from vegetation loss through over-grazing and leading to soil erosion, is rapidly rendering the dry range areas unproductive, and aiding the advance of deserts such as the Sahara. Many of these broad-scale assessments were based on early satellite imagery. This process of irreversible land degradation has been termed 'desertification', and a growing number of publications and conferences have examined the issue in some detail.

At the other end of the debate are those[13] who believe firstly that irreversible land degradation is not occurring to any great degree, and secondly that those who suggest that it is are merely disciples of Hardin's 'Tragedy of the Commons' thesis. While Hardin (1968) was in fact exploring the issues associated with the 'population problem', he used as his allegory the tragedy of the commons (public range), whereby herders seek to maximise their personal gain by increasing their herd size without limit, until the common grazing resource is completely destroyed. While Hardin was not specifically attempting to do so, he managed to give a reasonable representation of the nomadic behavioural model as perceived by Western rangeland scientists up until that time (and, for some, currently). The importance of this behavioural model is that, possibly more than any other single factor, it has helped to shape pastoral development interventions concerned with the modification of pastoralist behaviour.

The forces of change: redefining the problem of pastoral development

Firstly we must clarify what is encompassed by the term 'land degradation'. Land degradation has two components: vegetation degradation and soil degradation, which are closely interrelated. In general, range scientists argue that the avoidance of land degradation and the maintenance of long-term range productivity depend on maintaining ecosystem stability, or good range 'condition'. Preserving ecosystem stability involves several crucial factors:

- Maintaining an effective, protective, vegetative cover for the soil surface, particularly during dry periods. This requires a higher proportion of perennial (long-lived) plants than annual or ephemeral (short-lived) plants.

- Ensuring a high proportion of plants which are sufficiently palatable, digestible, and nutritious to maintain a grazing animal.

- Ensuring that the rate of soil erosion does not exceed the rate of soil formation. This means maintaining the (usually very thin) topsoil layer in range areas, and preventing the deterioration of the soil's structure and fertility.

A loss of range condition, or 'declining trend', can be characterised by any of the processes of soil erosion or soil-structural decline, a shift in plant-species composition away from palatable perennial plants towards annual or ephemeral plants, or a shift towards plants (perennial or annual) which are unpalatable, indigestible, or of low nutritional value. These processes are illustrated diagrammatically in Figure 2.1.

Relatively little is known of the vegetation biodynamics of dry-range ecosystems such as those of Africa and Australia. Traditional models of plant succession based on the Clementsian theory of plant ecology, which have historically dominated range-assessment procedures,[14] have recently come under criticism. Put simply, the Clementsian model of 'climax' community succession suggests that in response to variations in grazing pressure, range condition can be manipulated backwards and forwards from good to poor states along a graded continuum.

Empirical studies from a number of vegetation communities have challenged the 'climax community' model. These studies have shown that changes in range-condition trend may not be continuous or even reversible. Such observations have thrown up new theories of range ecology such as that of Westoby, Walker, and Noy-Meir (1989), which argues for a 'state-and-transition' model. In simple terms, this model suggests that range ecosystems may jump from one persistent state to

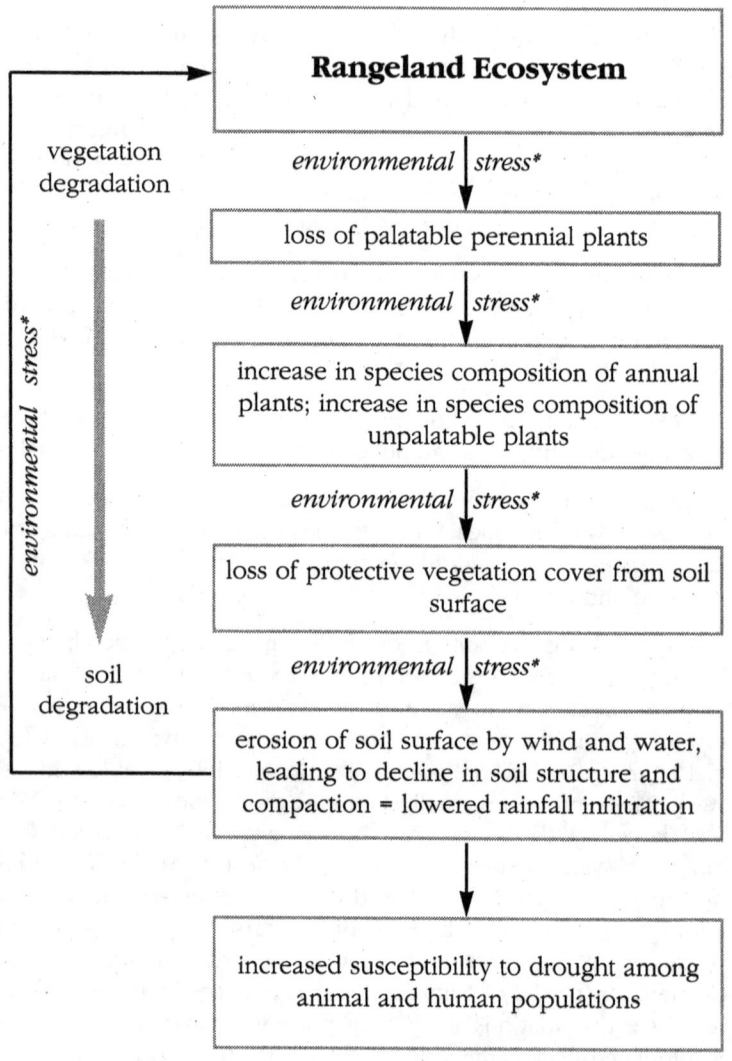

Figure 2.1: *The cycle of rangeland degradation and famine: an episodic and iterative process*

another persistent state. The 'transitions' between these states are triggered by natural events such as climatic changes (such as drought) or by management actions such as variations in stocking pressure or burning. The relevance of this model to the current discussion is that it predicts the following outcomes:

- Once a range vegetation has declined in condition to a particular state, the trend may not be reversible.

- Assumptions regarding a simple linear relationship between increases in grazing pressure and decline in range condition are often false. Under certain conditions (such as drought), even very low stocking rates may allow a transition to a lower-condition state, and under other conditions opportunistic heavy grazing may trigger a transition to a higher-condition state.[15]

These predictions directly contradict those of the Clementsian model. The importance of these contradictions lies in the fact that much of the range-assessment technology applied in the USA, and therefore in Africa, has been based on the Clementsian model of climax succession.

The above discussion highlights three important points in relation to the processes of land degradation as they occur in dry Africa:

- Vegetation degradation is a complex and subtle process.

- The measurement of vegetation degradation requires empirical studies that are specific to the ecosystem in question; assessments of pasture biomass alone, based on evidence such as that provided by satellite imagery, are poor indices of these processes.

- Within the African context, vegetation degradation may in some instances be irreversible.

The implications of these new models of range ecology for pastoral development policy are only now being explored.[16] There are three immediately evident outcomes of the new models. First, there is an increasing recognition of the wisdom of opportunistic grazing traditionally practised by transhumant pastoralists. Second, the concept that range areas have set livestock carrying capacities insensitive to seasonal fluctuations is increasingly being discarded. Third, the assumption driving many pastoral development interventions (that reducing livestock numbers would automatically lead to improvements in range condition) is now regarded as simplistic and in some circumstances invalid.

The question of the reversibility of accelerated soil erosion due to human impacts is easier to answer. When the rate of soil erosion exceeds the rate of soil formation to any significant degree, then it can be concluded that serious land degradation is occurring. Top-soil layers may take hundreds of years to re-form. Consequently, in terms of the human time-scale, severe soil erosion in dry areas should be considered an irreversible process.

Thus generalisations regarding trends in range condition and their reversibility, or otherwise, over large areas and over a variety of vegetation communities cannot be made with any reasonable degree of confidence in the absence of extensive ecological studies. Consequently, claims that much of sub-Saharan Africa is undergoing severe and rapid degradation of vegetation must be treated with some caution. Even in relatively well-studied African environments such as those of Zimbabwe, there is disagreement among observers about the extent and physical causes of land degradation.[17] Nevertheless, reports of severe soil erosion, an easily observable and essentially irreversible process, indicate that, at least in some countries, land degradation is a cause of major concern.

The probable primary causes of land degradation are socio-economic, demographic, and political in nature. These causes have already been discussed earlier in this chapter as individual entities. The loss of the better-quality range to other uses, the decreased mobility of pastoralists due to political boundaries or changes in land-tenure relationships, and pastoral population increases have acted together to produce marked increases in pastoral population densities. On one side of the pastoral balance sheet is a rapidly increasing subsistence requirement. On the other side of the balance sheet is a rapidly diminishing area of range available for pastoral use, and (due to land degradation within this available area) a diminishing proportion of that land which is productive. Suggested vertical and horizontal causal linkages between land degradation and the other forces of change are illustrated in Figure 2.2.

To describe land degradation as being caused by over-grazing by livestock is clearly an over-simplification. Over-grazing is simply the end-product of other forces operating higher up the causal chain. Designing development interventions to mitigate over-grazing is merely to treat a symptom of other processes. In the absence of development interventions directed at addressing these primary causes, projects designed to mitigate over-grazing are unlikely to prove successful over the longer term.

The forces of change: redefining the problem of pastoral development

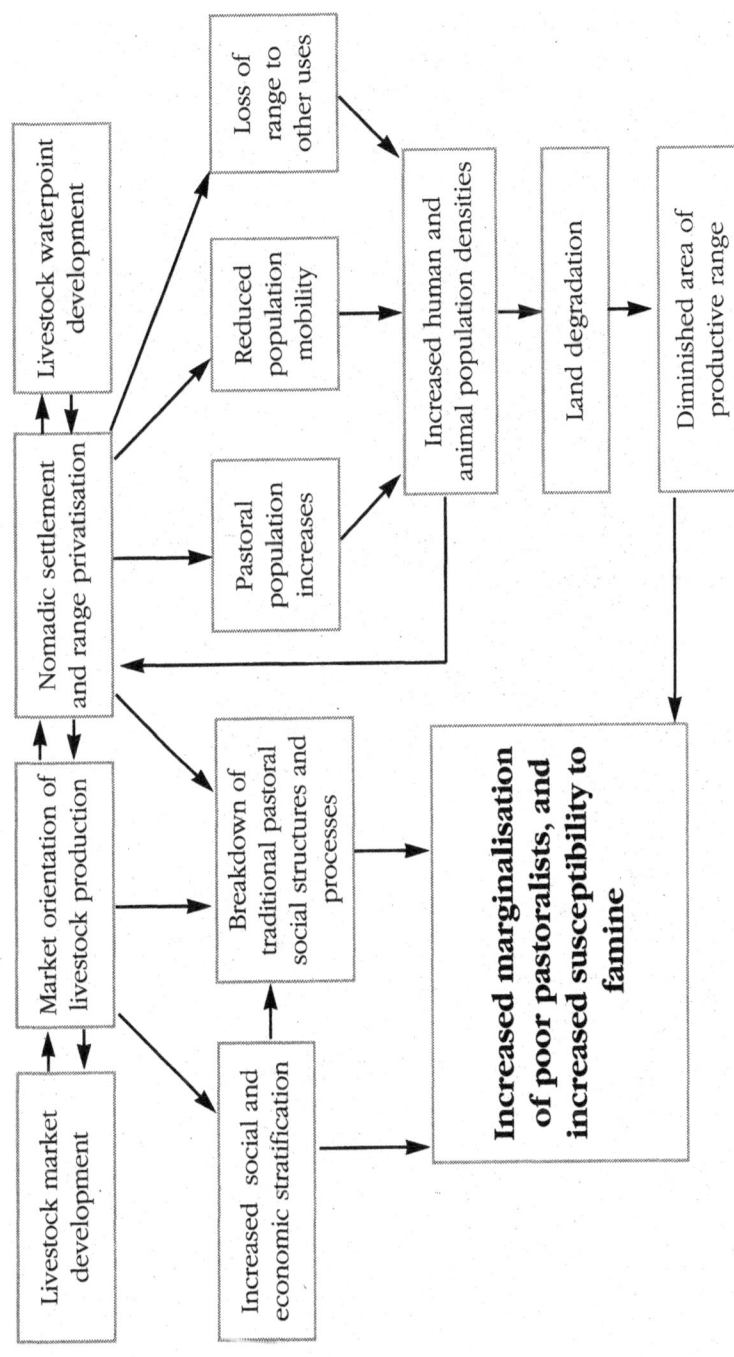

Figure 2.2: *The forces of change and suggested causal linkages within the pastoral sector*

Pastoral Development Planning

Sudan: a Beja nomad in the Red Sea Province

3

A critical review of the history of pastoral development projects

Introduction

If pastoral development experience has been less than impressive so far, we must ask whether it is possible to identify any consistency in the reasons for its poor record. This chapter attempts to do just that. By examining the literature on pastoral development projects, we will try to identify and categorise the reasons why project faults occur and recur. Secondly, we will seek potential solutions to these recurring programme shortcomings, so that these solutions may be translated into policies and strategies for programmes and projects.

Pastoral development projects may be categorised by the factors of the pastoral environment which they are trying to modify. Four categories, and some of their more common project forms, are listed below. Thus pastoral development interventions may seek to achieve one or more of the following:

- *Modification of the physical rangeland environment*: by means of interventions such as pasture improvement, soil and water conservation, livestock water-source development, and Tsetse fly eradication.

- *Modification of pastoralists' perceptions and actions*: through interventions like grazing controls, and pastoralist settlement through ranching schemes.

- *Improvements to the efficiency of pastoral production*: examples include livestock breeding programmes, livestock disease-control programmes, and improvements to the pastoral market economy.

- *Disaster mitigation*: development attempts at disaster mitigation are relatively recent and relatively uncommon. We will examine the record of famine-mitigation interventions, and post-drought restocking programmes.

The ensuing critical review of pastoral development projects highlights twelve commonly recurring project faults (see Table 3.1). Of these twelve, ten are internal to the local development environment, while two factors are external to it.

Table 3.1: Twelve commonly recurring factors contributing to the failure of pastoral development projects

Internal factors

a. Faults arising from a poor understanding of the pastoral development environment:
- Poor data base and inadequate definition of the problem
- Poor understanding of pastoralists' decision-making processes
- Generalisations about pastoral development environment
- A preoccupation with 'mainstream' notions of pastoralist behaviour

b. Faults within the development planning process:
- Faults inherent within the planning process itself
- Lack of development-planning skills among project personnel
- Failure to involve 'beneficiaries' in the planning process
- Neglect of institution building at both government and community levels

c. Faults attributable to poor project design:
- Faulty, unproven, or inappropriate technology
- Omission of goals related to justice and sustainability

External factors

a. Unfavourable policy environments created by indigenous governments

b. Intrusion of implicit organisational goals of development agencies and governments

Internal factors contributing to project failure

Most of the recurring faults which limit the success of pastoral development interventions are internal. That is, they are faults which are primarily caused by factors which are within the *local* development (or project) environment. This is an important point. In principle, local factors can be addressed by the nature of the design of the pastoral development intervention, or the nature of its implementation. They are not factors which are necessarily beyond the vision of project planners, nor are they necessarily beyond their ability to respond.

Faults arising from a poor understanding of the pastoral development environment

Four recurring faults can be attributed to a poor understanding of the pastoral development environment.

Poor data base and inadequate definition of the problem

A recurring theme within pastoral development interventions is the existence of a poor data base. Often the data fail to describe accurately either the causes or the scale of the problems of the pastoral sector. Inadequate data commonly result in two shortcomings:

- a tendency to underestimate the complex interacting forces in pastoral development environments;
- and a consequent tendency towards inadequate 'problem' definition, which results in project designs which address symptoms rather than causes.

A failure to recognise the complex interactions of the pastoral environment may mean that development interventions fail to achieve their development objectives, and they may also have undesirable unplanned impacts. Examples of interventions which commonly suffer from a poor understanding of the interactive nature of the pastoral environment include livestock water-point development, Tsetse-fly eradication programmes, ranching schemes, grazing-control schemes, and alterations to the pastoral economy.

Development attempts to construct new wells for livestock watering have often succeeded in intensifying grazing pressures and damaging the range ecology.[1] Such developments have also sparked off conflict, often violent, between pastoralists themselves or between pastoralists and government workers.[2] Nevertheless, well-construction remains a popular development option in many countries.

The Food and Agriculture Organisation of the United Nations (FAO) estimates that African cattle production could effectively be doubled with the eradication of Tsetse fly.[3] While prophylactic trypanocide drugs are available for cattle, their protection is incomplete and their cost high. Consequently pastoral development interventions have focused on efforts to eradicate the Tsetse fly. Such measures in the past have concentrated on the killing of over a million wild animals thought to harbour the disease, the clear felling of large areas of the bush habitat of the Tsetse fly, and the application of chlorinated hydrocarbon insecticides. All these methods proved to be very destructive to the environment. More recently, insect pheromones have been utilised in conjunction with traps impregnated with contact insecticides, and traps coloured to attract the insects have been designed to kill them with solar heat.

However, there are environmental and social costs associated with the changes in land use enabled by eradicating the Tsetse fly. Eradication without concomitant controls on land use may contribute to subsequent over-grazing, in much the same way as does the construction of a permanent watering point in a new area. There is not time for land users to institute customary pastoral land-use controls, designed to avoid over-grazing, in areas recently rendered Tsetse-free, before land degradation results.[4] Breeding programmes designed to produce trypano-tolerant cattle[5] carry the same inherent dangers of encouraging over-grazing, if not accompanied by appropriate controls on land use.

It is not only in the area of unplanned physical impacts that Tsetse-eradication programmes have encountered problems. A poor social and political data base in relation to one Tsetse-eradication programme in central Somalia allowed well-connected government officials to annexe the new higher-value Tsetse-free land from the traditional pastoralists and agro-pastoralists.[6]

Ranching schemes have been a widespread and relatively unsuccessful intervention in the pastoral sector. The adoption of ranching schemes as an appropriate development intervention was based on a number of assumptions about the perceived shortcomings of the traditional land-use systems of nomadic and communal pastoral societies. A fundamental assumption was that traditional pastoral management systems were less economically productive than the ranching model. The definition of economic productivity used in making this assumption was based on the off-take from herds of animals for the market. Recent comparisons of productivity have included the subsistence

A critical review of the history of pastoral development projects

production (milk, meat, and skins consumed, and breeding and draught animals retained and not sold) of both management systems. These studies have concluded that traditional systems are in fact more productive than ranching schemes.[7]

Interventions which attempt to modify the pastoral market economy also suffer from inadequate data. Often these developments were based on assumptions which were the result of belief rather than rigorous observation. Not surprisingly, the history of market interventions has been one of considerable failure. Market interventions are often little more than exercises in the application of economic theory, and display a poor understanding of the social or economic system being manipulated.

The issue of government intervention and price controls, and their relationship to the supply of livestock products to the market, has received substantial attention. In particular, such market interventions suffer from a poor understanding of the factors affecting pastoralists' decisions to sell their animals. One of the most vexing tasks for those wishing to 'improve' the pastoral market economy through development intervention is the effort needed to understand the nature of pastoralists' supply responses to changes in the prices of their products. Empirical studies have shown that the process of deciding whether or not to sell is complex and still poorly understood.

Doran, Low, and Kemp (1979) found that, of the between-year variations in the supply of market animals in Swaziland, 40 per cent could be attributed to price changes, 25 per cent to rainfall fluctuations, and 35 per cent to unidentified factors. Subsequently, Low (1980) identified the status of the herd inventory (herd size, age, and gender ratio) as being a major contributor to this trend. Low suggested that, in order to explain changes in supply over time, it is also necessary to quantify changes in the livestock inventory over the same period. Thus when herds are decimated by drought, the immediate post-drought supply of livestock to the market would be low, whatever the price being offered. Conversely, if high prices encouraged pastoralists to add to their herds over time, then the supply to the market would continue to be high, relatively independent of price movements — until the herd size had been reduced.

Thus it is difficult to predict pastoralists' supply responses to price changes for their livestock commodities, even over relatively small areas and limited time scales. No universal proposition can be put forward which accurately describes the relationship between livestock price and livestock supply. So it is not surprising that where price controls have been implemented, usually through government parastatals, they have frequently achieved results which were contrary to the stated objectives of the intervention.

Sullivan (1984), in reviewing the experiences in Ghana and Tanzania of government market-control interventions, found the efforts to be counterproductive to efficient market operations. In the early 1970s both governments instituted marketing organisations which controlled the purchase and market distribution of livestock and set livestock price-ceilings at a low level, designed to satisfy the politically more powerful urban consumers. In Ghana the government undervalued meat to a level half that of the free-market price. This led to a reduction of livestock supply to the market, forcing the importation of beef for the domestic market. In Tanzania pastoralists responded to the forced low prices by illegally exporting animals across the borders into neighbouring countries. By 1979 both countries had experienced collapse in the livestock market. Bekure and McDonald (1985: 5) cite similar examples of price-control schemes which failed in Uganda, Kenya, Zaire, and Sudan.

Despite the fact that market interventions continue, several authors have questioned the need for any outside interventions in the livestock market economy. Sandford (1983: 199-229), in his general analysis of African livestock markets, concludes that:

• The free-market system in the form most commonly found in African pastoral markets operates with considerable efficiency and rarely requires outside interventions to improve its operations.

• Overland trekking of market livestock in its traditional form is the lowest-cost alternative (both in direct money terms and in terms of livestock mortality and 'shrinkage'), when compared with road and truck transport.

• Government interventions in the pastoral marketplace have been inappropriate, with the possible exception of the occasions when official institutions have been used to purchase livestock during drought-induced crises.

• The construction and location of abattoirs provide a significant opportunity for the implementation of government policy, particularly in relation to pricing policy, where a monopoly position can allow government to keep livestock prices artificially high (as was the case in Botswana) or artificially low (as occurred in Tanzania).

A critical review of the history of pastoral development projects

Evangelou (1984), in his analysis of local livestock-market operations in Kenyan Maasailand, drew conclusions similar to those of Sandford. Evangelou found the markets to be reasonably efficient, and the trekking method of stock transport less costly than that of trucking. He concluded that improvements to the market system under observation would be achieved only if (firstly) producers became more market-oriented and could therefore achieve consistency in supply, and (secondly) the national government's pricing policies were more accurately to reflect demand.

Grazing controls are commonly included as components of pastoral development projects, normally in the form of rotational grazing schemes or destocking programmes. One goal of grazing controls is usually the improvement of range condition through the removal of grazing pressure. In the absence of empirical support, this improvement in range condition is often assumed. However, it is impossible to predict accurately the response of botanical composition (or animal productivity) to variations in either the grazing period or the grazing intensity, without first carrying out experimental studies. Such studies of range condition and trend must be long-term and considered relatively site-specific. It is a mistake to assume changes in range condition, in either a positive or negative direction, in the absence of empirical data. Both US and Australian studies suggest that variations in botanical composition in response to rotational grazing systems are ecosystem-specific, and therefore unpredictable.[9] The classical theory about rangeland ecology is that with increasing grazing pressure there is a decrease in the population of palatable perennial plants and an increase in the population of short-lived annuals and unpalatable perennial plants (weeds). While such relationships have been observed in many ecological studies, other studies have identified different trends altogether.[10]

Thus a number of types of pastoral development were based upon empirically unverified assumptions or beliefs. This in part explains the poor record of some of these interventions. Another explanation of the poor development record in this area relates to the limited scope of the data base and the limited scope of the definition of the development 'problem' being addressed. Often within project design the 'problem' is defined in physical terms, which means that the proposed solution depends on the implementation of technical measures. Yet there is increasing evidence[11] to suggest that the primary causes of the highly visible physical problems of the pastoral sector are in fact non-physical — that is social, economic, and political.

To take over-grazing, vegetation loss, and soil erosion as examples: in project design these physical 'problems' are usually addressed by technical measures such as grazing reserves, destocking, ranching schemes, or soil-conservation structural works. Commonly the causes of these degradation problems are attributed to communal land-tenure or too many grazing livestock. Yet communal systems of land tenure have operated in nomadic pastoral areas for thousands of years. Serious land degradation in the majority of areas now of concern is less than one hundred years old. Consequently the causes of land degradation must lie not in any particular communal system of land tenure *per se*, but in other forces of change, described in the previous chapter, which have come into operation during this century.

Poor understanding of pastoralists' decision-making processes

Many pastoral project interventions plan either to utilise, or to influence, pastoralists' decision-making processes. This may be attempted through modifying pastoralists' perceptions or their actions, or both. Yet the intention to achieve behavioural change through influencing pastoralists' decision-making processes often remains unrecognised in project-design documents. So the manner in which information, perceptions, values, and norms interact in the decision-making process is rarely researched.

For example, soil and water conservation (SWC) projects often seek to modify pastoralists' behaviour in a number of ways. Frequently pastoralists and agro-pastoralists are called upon to maintain SWC structures (commonly diversionary or contour bunds) once the bulldozers have departed. Several observers[12] have noted the subsequent failure of beneficiaries to maintain structures, and the consequent failure of the works within a relatively short time. It has been suggested[13] that this failure is explained by two key factors which influence pastoralists' decisions about how to allocate labour. Firstly, maintenance of SWC structures must compete with herding activities in the allocation of labour. Thus pastoralists prefer low-maintenance structures (rock bunds, small earth bunds), rather than the high-maintenance, bulldozer-constructed large earth bunds. Secondly, in order to invest labour in the maintenance of SWC structures, pastoralists and agro-pastoralists must feel that they have security of land tenure. This security of tenure, and the resultant sense of ownership of SWC structures, is not usually the concern of implementing agencies.

Livestock water-source development is another form of intervention which suffers from ignorance of pastoralists' decision-making

Somalia: of all the sources of conflict over natural resources throughout dry pastoral Africa, the control of water is perhaps the most highly politicised.

processes. Of all the sources of conflict over natural resources throughout dry pastoral Africa, water — its abundance, location, and control — is perhaps the most highly politicised. Pastoral development interventions involving water development must not only confront the ecological and technical issues, but must also take into account the intervention's impacts upon the socio-political environment. Water-source developers have repeatedly ignored the socio-political significance of water and its critical influence upon pastoralists' decision making. Often this lack of understanding has resulted in bloody and fatal conflict, destruction of pumping equipment, and the degradation of the surrounding land.[14]

In the past, ranching schemes have been plagued first by an ignorance of the importance of the subsistence needs of pastoralists (which results in failed projects), and second by the failure to recognise indigenous social units and kinship ties (which can result in violent conflict). All these factors have a significant bearing on pastoralists' decision making.[15] Ranching schemes have also failed to recognise pastoralists' needs for mobility and the maintenance of kinship ties, both important tools for risk-spreading.

Stock-reduction schemes suffered from a similar failure to recognise the multiple values attributed to livestock by African pastoralists. Pastoralists of the Erigavo District in North-West Somalia (Somaliland), for example, attribute values to their livestock which include capital, subsistence, disaster mitigation, maintenance of kinship ties, religious contract, and social values — among others (Prior 1992a). These values almost entirely relate to risk-spreading mechanisms in an uncertain environment. Pastoralists' livestock-management decisions will be based on assessments related to this cluster of values. Stock-reduction schemes which fail to recognise the broader social and political significance of livestock, and which do not attempt to compensate for the loss of these broader benefits, will always be resisted by pastoralists. The complex property rights and social contracts attached to livestock also pose problems for post-drought restocking schemes which are intent on treating livestock solely as a transferable economic commodity (Burke 1990).

Greater attention should be given at both the data-gathering and project-design phases to the development of robust descriptive models of pastoralist decision-making processes. Such models should be used predictively to judge the probable success of planned project impacts, as well as to identify the likelihood and nature of unplanned impacts resulting from the intervention.

A tendency to generalise about pastoral planning environments

Within the pastoral development arena there is a strong tendency on the part of both practitioners and theorists to generalise about pastoral planning environments, despite the variations in cultures, economies, politics, and histories which occur in pastoral Africa.

Generalisations in the theoretical literature may be justifiable in terms of defining pastoral 'paradigms'. However, when such generalisations also dictate the nature and form of development interventions, as occurred in the case of ranching schemes designed to mitigate range degradation and increase market off-take of livestock, or permanent water-source development to 'open up the range', it was hardly a recipe for success. There are few countries in sub-Saharan Africa where these forms of intervention have not been imposed at one time or another. Yet even between pastoral tribes living within the geographical boundaries of one country there may be extreme variations in cultures, economies, politics, and histories.

A preoccupation with 'mainstream' notions of pastoralist behaviour

One particular form of generalisation deserves special attention. This is the historical preoccupation of people trained in the field of range science with the 'mainstream' model (as coined by Sandford 1983: 11-18) of pastoralist behaviour. This model assumed that pastoralists are uniformly and habitually 'livestock maximisers', who are largely indifferent to the land degradation that is occurring around them. This picture essentially mirrors Hardin's 'Tragedy of the Commons' argument (Hardin 1968).

Many international observers accept the notion that land-degradation processes are somehow causally linked with the social organisation of pastoral cultures, and with the values and production goals inherently expressed by these organisations. The belief that pastoralist behaviour is *inherently* self-destructive over the longer term, through its negative impacts on the range environment, was constructed from the following 'axioms':

- that pastoralists strive to maximise their animal numbers because of some cultural fascination with their grazing animals (for instance, the 'cattle complex' of the Karamajong of Uganda and the Masaai of Kenya,[16] or the 'camel complex' of the Somalis);

- that pastoralists maximise their animal numbers because they view them as a repository of wealth or capital;[17]

- that pastoralists are unaware of, or discount, the land degradation they are causing, particularly when it entails the destruction of communal range over which they hold no individual title;[18]

- that pastoral nomadism is an economically and ecologically inefficient form of production, and that replacement by sedentary pastoral systems such as ranching is desirable;[19]

- that both pastoralists and their animals are increasing in number to the degree where in many areas they have exceeded the carrying capacity of the range on which they depend.[20]

As a consequence of these 'axioms', pastoralist behaviour was judged to be irrational, economically inefficient, and environmentally destructive. A number of pastoral development approaches were based on the assumption that pastoralists are primarily concerned with maximising their herd numbers. This viewpoint also assumed that pastoralists were seemingly unconcerned with the extreme rates of land degradation that confronted them, so long as the land did not belong to them. Development interventions thus tried to modify these 'unproductive' nomadic behavioural patterns, in deference to the 'productive' Western sedentary model.

Recently the concept of the irrational, unproductive, and self-destructive nomadic pastoralist has come under strong challenge. The first point of contention is the emerging view that vague generalised models of the social behaviour of widely disparate nomadic cultures are of little use, and should be considered structurally and predictively weak. As a result of specific studies of the social organisation of a number of nomadic cultures, the following viewpoints have emerged which contradict the early behavioural models and the conclusions which were drawn from them:

- that the often-observed land degradation is not the direct result of the inherent characteristics of nomadic behaviour, but rather reflects the inability of existing social organisations to adapt to abnormal circumstances;[21]

- that in many pastoralist cultures livestock are not utilised merely as repositories of wealth, but have a complex of values and needs attached to them,[22] and consequently the maximisation of animal numbers is unlikely to be a goal in itself;[23]

- that there is now sufficient evidence of instances where individuals jointly and wisely manage commonly owned lands over long periods (thus challenging the 'Tragedy of the Commons' axiom[24]), although the debate remains intense;[25]

- that nomadic stock-raising is an ecologically efficient way in which to utilise the arid or semi-arid ecosystem, where the availability of rainfall and pasture is extremely variable;[26]

- that the productivity of nomadic stock-raising may be at least equal to that of sedentary grazing systems, once the subsistence value of production (such as milk and hides) is added to the market value of production.[27]

Whether or not the 'mainstream' view of pastoralist behaviour is a valid descriptive model is not the central question here, though (as suggested) there is increasing evidence that at least in some environments it is not. What is open to challenge is the influence of this model on the definitions of pastoral problems, their causes and solutions, which ultimately dictated the form of project interventions attempted.

A critical review of the history of pastoral development projects

Faults within the development planning process

Four recurring faults can be identified which are attributable to particular characteristics of the development planning process.

Faults inherent within the planning process itself

A common recurring model of larger development interventions involves a comprehensive 'top-down' project design. This design incorporates a relatively complex series of interdependent, quantitatively defined objectives, the achievement of which will be quantitatively evaluated. The achievement of each of these objectives will have a time scale defined in the original design. Often the success or failure of one objective will determine the achievement (or otherwise) of another dependent objective.

This model fails to recognise a dynamic system and lacks inherent flexibility. The pastoral planning environment may experience rapid climatic, political, and economic changes. The environment being planned for at the stage of initial data collection and project design may have changed dramatically by the time of, and during, the implementation phase. By the stage of project evaluation, the intervention may be either irrelevant or antagonistic to the solution of the problem being addressed.

One reviewer argues that 'Project goals need to be thought of as hypotheses to be tested, not as scientific predictions' (Gall 1982: 74). The pastoral planning environment is inherently complex. Given the relatively poor data base upon which many projects are founded, and the fact that the collection of some forms of data can take place only at certain times and in certain seasons, many projects are designed with a poor understanding of the environment being manipulated. It is impossible to predict the outcomes of many planning initiatives with any accuracy. Objectives which are rigidly defined and given finite completion dates at the start of the project, without allowing for later modification, are more likely to lead to failure. Where the achievements of a number of objectives are interdependent, the non-achievement of one objective can cause the non-achievement of others. Often individual objectives are complex and over-optimistic in relation to the constraints of the planning environment. Such a planning approach is fragile.

Data collection should not finish with project design. The implementation phase is also an opportunity for data gathering, whereby on-going monitoring and feedback allow for a continuing learning process. The lessons gleaned from this process should be

Pastoral Development Planning

Tarbaj, Kenya, December 1992: Oxfam Programme Officer, Youssuf Mutar, visits one of 30 women-headed households restocked by Oxfam in 1984. He has followed up each family, providing veterinary support and advice, on regular walking tours through the bush.

utilised to redefine and modify project objectives and implementation procedures.

This style of development planning could be described as the 'process approach', rather than the 'project approach'. The intervention's chances of success are strengthened by adopting a flexible and responsive approach, in contrast to the comprehensive, rigid, overcomplex, and often technocratic traditional approach to development planning. Nevertheless, process approaches such as that proposed by Korten (1980) have been almost completely absent from government-implemented pastoral development projects in Africa.

The adoption of a process approach to pastoral development by definition requires that the details of project design are incrementally derived over time. Thus the project personnel who manage and implement development must by definition be able to contribute to project design. This avoids one of the major factors contributing to faulty project design. By ensuring that those who design the project are the same people who will have to implement it, it is possible to avoid many of the problems created when unimplementable strategies, or unachievable objectives, are incorporated into project-design documents.

A lack of development planning skills among project personnel

At least some of the failures of pastoral development projects can be attributed to inherent faults in the planning process. Inevitably this fact raises doubts about the skills of those carrying out the planning.

Commonly those people who are charged with the design and implementation of pastoral development projects are chosen from technical fields related to the nature of the physical, social, or economic problem being addressed. Often these people have no formal training in development planning, but some have considerable development experience, acquired through their tenure on past projects. However, in the absence of formal training in development planning, such supposedly experienced people will often fail to recognise the variety of different development planning approaches from which to choose, and are not likely to examine their previous project involvement critically. Consequently, they tend to reproduce past mistakes with each subsequent project.

An example of a narrow technical viewpoint is found in a recent FAO publication dealing with soil and water conservation in semi-arid areas. This 150-page technical document[28] devotes only one page to a consideration of the importance of the human factor in project planning. The author admits that in order to enhance a project's chances of success,

> it is increasingly recognised that a complete understanding is required of all the social and economic ramifications of the farming system in order to guide component research into topics and techniques which will be applicable.

However, the publication does not go on to consider these important points in any detail. What is more, viewing human factors as valid research topics is a long way from actually doing participatory development. A tendency to exclude and ignore key facets of the development environment which do not fall within the boundaries of one's technical specialism is not restricted to soil and water conservation projects. It is just as commonplace in projects with an economic focus as it is with those concerned with physical development. In such cases disciplinary 'professionalism' becomes a major obstacle to participatory development. Development planning must be seen as a pluralistic activity where the bio-physical vigorously interacts with the socio-economic and political. This requires of development practitioners a broader perspective and understanding that substantially exceeds that of the narrow technical focus often demanded in project-design documents.

On the other hand, while tertiary training in development planning is now available at a number of Western universities, and in time should also become more common in African institutions, the tendency is to turn out development planning professionals with few technical skills. Consequently they are rarely employed on projects or project components which are seen as technical in nature. So those in technical fields need also to gain training in development planning. However, the impetus for this transformation should come initially from the employing agencies themselves, which must demand personnel with both technical and development planning skills.

Failure to involve 'beneficiaries' in the development planning process

In some instances project failure has largely been attributed to the target population's lack of involvement in the planning process. Historically, large-scale mechanised SWC projects viewed the local people as 'beneficiaries' of, rather than 'participants' in, the development process. At the design stage, planners commonly fail to consult the local population about their goals and needs, or the existence of traditional SWC methodologies; indeed, they fail to credit them with any views at all about what a SWC project should entail. The implementation phase, in which soil-conservation engineers and bulldozers roll through the landscape, moulding it catchment by catchment, is viewed with bewilderment, concern, or even anger by the local population. On several occasions it has been noted that 'beneficiaries' have destroyed or modified earthworks soon after the bulldozers have departed, because the remaining structures did not fit their view of worthwhile development.[29]

When the local people are excluded from the development decision-making process, they cannot be simply slotted into the implementation phase of a project because of an *ad hoc* project design made in the absence of community consultation. Not surprisingly, when beneficiaries are called upon to maintain large machinery-constructed bunds, they often refuse, because they believe that those responsible for the construction of the structures should also be responsible for their maintenance.[30] On occasions when beneficiaries were involved in the decision making, they demonstrated a willingness to maintain SWC structures which they themselves constructed and over which they felt they had some ownership.[31]

A critical review of the history of pastoral development projects

Similarly, a failure to involve beneficiaries in the development planning process contributed to the failure of other types of interventions such as rotational grazing schemes (Spencer 1973) and ranching schemes (Oxby 1985). On the other hand, many paraveterinary projects both involve the beneficiaries in the decision making and attempt to meet a high-priority need.[32] While there are still a number of problems associated with paraveterinary projects (see, for example, Zeissan 1986), many were successful.

For example, Oxfam (UK and Ireland), in association with the Sudanese NGO ACCOMPLISH, has co-ordinated a programme of training and support to paravets selected from the Mundari community in Terekeka District north of Juba town — an area ravaged by civil war, and consequently with severe animal-health problems. The training for the paravets lasts for four to five weeks; they are equipped with a bicycle and a box of equipment, and the drugs are kept in portable kerosene fridges; they are paid on a daily basis when on vaccination duty. The programme has concentrated on two areas: vaccination of cattle against epizootic diseases (Rinderpest and Contagious Bovine Pleuro Pneumonia) and the control of an epidemic of Bovine Theileriosis, specifically East Coast Fever, which

Sudan: Oxfam-funded Mundari paravet vaccinating cattle against East Coast fever.

was discovered by the project in 1986. By 1989 almost 400,000 head had been vaccinated and over 2,000 successfully treated for East Coast Fever. This service is very popular, and demand for it outstrips the capacity of the project. The availability of vaccines and drugs has apparently quelled some hostilities between local factions, as everyone knows that an unstable political situation would threaten the existence of this community-oriented veterinary service.[33]

Significantly, a failure to involve beneficiaries in the development planning process, particularly at the level of problem definition, has also meant that certain types of interventions have not been attempted. In particular there is a lack of development interventions (as opposed to relief efforts or monitoring frameworks) designed to mitigate and avoid natural events such as drought and disasters such as famine. Recent policy reviews by government bodies give insufficient emphasis to this issue (Sandford 1985; UN Economic Commission for Africa 1985). Where policy documents have touched upon the need for food security (for example World Bank 1989a), they have failed to grapple with the detail of how this might be achieved.

African pastoralists are intensely concerned with risk-spreading. Pastoralists live in an environment which may be subject to immense climatic, political, and economic fluctuations. Faced with such variability, pastoralists spread the potential impacts of future risks through such mechanisms as transhumance and seasonal grazing, opportunistic agriculture, livestock diversification, and the maintenance of kinship ties. For these groups the greatest fear commonly expressed is that of severe drought. Oba and Lusigi (1987) offer a review of indigenous pastoral mechanisms for coping with drought; but these mechanisms are of only limited use in mitigating droughts which are long-lasting and widespread.

Two issues are therefore of primary importance to pastoral groups: first, the avoidance of drought and subsequent famine; and second, the employment of potential post-drought recovery mechanisms. Yet despite the fact that drought mitigation seems to be a commonly expressed need of pastoral communities, virtually no projects specifically designed to address this need have been established until the last few years. Even now, apart from a few attempts at setting up Famine Early Warning Systems (FEWS), it is not the larger multilateral or bilateral agencies or even indigenous governments which in general are attempting such interventions with any frequency (although there have been exceptions in Botswana[34]). Rather it is the smaller NGOs which have done so.

A critical review of the history of pastoral development projects

Gir Gir Group Ranch, Samburu District, Kenya: Mary, widowed in 1991, received 20 goats in 1992 from the local Oxfam-funded Restocking Committee. All the animals had been repaid by earlier beneficiaries.

In particular, two types of intervention designed to meet pastoralists' need for disaster mitigation have attracted the attention of NGOs. These are cereal storage banks and post-drought restocking programmes. Efforts to develop cereal banks have encountered problems, though there are examples of successful community cereal banks.[35] Post-drought restocking programmes are designed to prevent the poorer marginalised pastoralists being forced to abandon pastoralism and seek other economic activities for which they are generally ill-prepared. Displaced pastoralists who do not become dependants in refugee camps may end up on the peripheries of larger urban centres, swelling the populations of slum areas. The experience of post-drought restocking programmes, although still limited, suggests that this form of intervention, if properly designed and implemented, can aid poorer pastoralists during times of stress.[36]

Because of the limit to the number of livestock that can be bought and held ready for redistribution in any one area, restocking projects have in most cases been small-scale initiatives supported by NGOs. Oxfam (UK and Ireland) has particular experience in this field: the Habbanae Project (Abala, Niger) restocked some 350 WoDaaBe families who had been badly hit by the 1972-73 drought; and a series of

41

restocking projects was set up in Kenya, in response to the 1983-84 drought there: 70 Boran families were restocked in Isiolo District, 30 in Wajir District, 380 in Turkana District, and 186 in Samburu District. These numbers include a varying proportion of female-headed families, except in the case of Wajir, where all the heads of families were female (mostly women widowed as a result of civil war).

These projects have typically distributed to each family a herd of livestock, most usually between 30 and 70 goats; food in the form of the local grain staple, until the herds have begun to grow; and a pack animal, usually a donkey, to fetch the food. Veterinary assistance has been provided in the early stages. Two major attractions of restocking are (first) that no training is required, since the beneficiaries are already experienced in herding; and (second) that environmental pressure on the congested settlement areas is relieved, since project beneficiaries are required to take their newly acquired herds away to remoter, under-used pastures. (For further information about restocking projects, see Toulmin 1986, Fry 1988, and Oxby 1989.)

Participatory development can really be achieved only on a small scale at any one time. This is because project officers have to develop a good understanding of, and effective rapport with, the communities with whom they are dealing. They must also identify the target population and ensure that it is they who participate in the decision making. It is axiomatic that, within any community, those with greatest access to channels of communication and resources are the more powerful elites. There is a need to ensure that those who are targeted, say the poorer families, have effective access to the process of participation.

The final problem relates to how we actually define what is meant by the term 'participation'. Arnstein (1969), for example, defines eight degrees of so-called participation which vary from 'manipulation' of beneficiaries by the planning agency through to 'citizen control', whereby the beneficiaries alone make the planning decisions. Needless to say, in the pastoral development planning arena we have seen many examples of the former, and little of the latter. Participatory development is a complex issue and often difficult to achieve. As the Erigavo case study later in this book demonstrates, participation may often involve an evolutionary process which progresses as the organisational capacity of local beneficiaries increases, and greater control over the development process is devolved to the beneficiaries.

There are potential disadvantages in encouraging participatory approaches: project appraisal may take longer, and cost more. Often project designs merely pay lip service to participation. Nevertheless, broad reviews of the experience of participatory approaches to rural development have come out strongly in their favour.[37]

Recently there has also been recognition, especially among NGOs, of the need to incorporate into project design indigenous mechanisms for problem identification and problem solution ('indigenous technical knowledge').[38] Interventions which build on indigenous mechanisms tend to be more acceptable to participating communities, and are more likely to be sustainable.

Neglect of institution-building at government and community levels

Large projects funded by multilateral and bilateral agencies are commonly carried out in conjunction with an indigenous government institution. When the external agency departs from the project, the government institution is expected to carry on the project's activities with or without some form of on-going agency support. Frequently, the intervention technology chosen for this type of project is relatively complex, with high recurrent costs. So after the departure of the donor agency, the eventual long-term success of the project depends on the indigenous government institution's ability to absorb the project activities, technically, financially, and administratively.

The isolation of pastoral areas places extra administrative and logistical burdens on indigenous governments. It is not uncommon for the project activities of indigenous government to collapse completely soon after the external agency's support has (prematurely) come to an end. This has particularly been the case with soil and water conservation interventions.[39]

The absorptive capacity of government institutions is therefore a fundamental determinant of a project's longer-term success. Yet this aspect of project design has been neglected by development planners until relatively recently. One probable reason for this omission is the fact that until recently the sustainability of project activities after the donor's departure was rarely included as an objective in design documents.

Morss, Gow, and Nordlinger (1985: 218) suggest three general factors which hinder the capacity of a government institution to absorb on-going project activities following the withdrawal of the donor's support. These are:

- *financial factors*, involving the employment of expensive project technologies with high recurrent costs and low revenue-generation;

- *political and economic factors*, especially unfavourable government policies and low political support for the project relative to other competing activities;
- *institutional factors*, relating to the organisational weakness, both administratively and politically, of some government ministries.

The same writers suggest a number of possible ways to improve the absorptive capacity of government organisations. Perhaps the most crucial of these is the need for donor agencies to recognise the importance of institution-building within their initial project design, and ensure that enough time and resources are allowed to achieve it.

One type of development which avoids the institutional weakness of indigenous government departments is the so-called 'community development' approach often employed by NGOs. Community development seeks to utilise low-cost simple technologies, commonly using locally available materials. The beneficiaries themselves, rather than government employees, are trained in the technologies, in the hope that they will be able to sustain the project activities once external support has ended. However, community-development approaches do not avoid all of the problems of absorptive capacity encountered by the larger projects which involve government agencies. Many a community-development project has foundered because of a lfailure to recognise of the huge variation in organisational skills to be found in different communities. Some communities have well-developed decision-making procedures for consensus seeking and group action, but others do not.

Community development involves building up the organisational skills of the beneficiaries as much as (or, on occasion, more than) it involves transferring technology. The capacity of a group or community to organise itself does not only determine its ability to institute technological development. The ability to organise also allows the community to confront adverse environmental forces more effectively as a group, as well as to strengthen its position in the political decision-making process which determines the allocation of resources. The same also applies to disadvantaged sub-sets within a community, such as the poor, or women and girls.

Faults attributable to poor project design

Some failures in pastoral development projects can be attributed to faults inherent within project design. We will consider two categories of faulty project design, both very broad in their scope.

Faulty, unproven, or inappropriate technology

All forms of project intervention are susceptible to the employment of unsuitable technology, although some types of intervention in particular seem more prone than others. Some forms which appear to be endemically afflicted with a poor choice of technology include projects involving large machinery-constructed soil and water conservation structures (expensive to install and maintain); certain Tsetse-fly eradication efforts (environmentally destructive); ranching schemes (ecologically inappropriate); grazing reserves (based on unproven ecological assumptions); and permanent water-source development involving bores (which are environmentally destructive, and rely on unsustainable pumping devices).

Yet, despite a growing body of literature describing inappropriate technologies, a number continue to be implemented, often because they are regarded as easy development. For example, while there has been a gradual, though belated, recognition among policy-makers of the environmental folly in indiscriminate development of permanent watering points, development agencies continue to be attracted to this form of intervention. The Central Rangelands Development Project (CRDP) in central Somalia (funded by the World Bank and implemented by the Somali government) planned for extensive development of boreholes in the original design documents. However, project staff recognised the pitfalls of such an approach and abandoned them in favour of earth-dugout construction. The dugouts would supply water for only limited periods of the year, so that grazing of the range areas serviced by them would be restricted to those periods.[40] Yet when this writer visited the CRDP area in 1987, two years after the borehole-construction programme had been abandoned, project staff had just discovered to their surprise that another borehole-drilling project, funded by an Arab Gulf government, had begun operations in the CRDP project area. The borehole-construction project had failed to consult the CRDP staff and had in fact constructed boreholes at sites which the CRDP had judged to be environmentally vulnerable.

In 1988 in northern Somalia the writer observed the start of two borehole-drilling projects, one funded by an NGO and the other by a European government. Neither project employed any staff with training in the conservation of rangeland ecology, nor did they appear to be aware of the extreme rangeland degradation associated with previous well-construction schemes in the region. In both cases, project policy was to rely on the advice of district and regional government officials and local community elders to identify appropriate locations for bore sites.

Finally, water — its abundance, location, and control — is perhaps the most highly politicised source of conflict over resources throughout dry pastoral Africa. Any pastoral development intervention involving water development must not only confront the ecological and technical issues, but also take into account the impact which the intervention will have upon the socio-political environment.

Seizure and control of a well by one pastoral group to the exclusion of others is not an uncommon ploy in dry areas. This may occur when available pasture is diminishing, at the end of the dry season or during a drought. It may also be used to claim not pasture as such but land. This process was observed by the writer on several occasions in the Erigavo District of North-West Somalia/Somaliland. The process of sedentarisation of nomadic communities and the consequent privatisation of formerly public range resulted on several occasions in opposing groups claiming the ownership of wells also formerly in the public domain. The seizure of the wells allowed the controlling groups to lay claim to the lands within grazing distance of the water points. Following the start of the Somali civil war in May 1988 and the ensuing inter-tribal conflict, Jidali Well near Erigavo was seized by tribal groups supporting the government military forces, to the exclusion of other tribes who supported the opposition forces. This action occurred in the middle of the wet season, when access to pasture was not an issue. The seizure of the well was both an act of political will in the most traditional of manners and a natural pragmatic response by pastoralists to a period of insecurity.

This is not to reject completely the construction of permanent watering points: under particular circumstances they may be appropriate. However, in planning borehole locations, consideration must be given to current rangeland condition and probable future condition, given an intensification of grazing pressure. Consideration must also be given to the potential for future government or community controls on grazing, either directly or indirectly (through controls on water use), and the likely impact on local political relationships of the construction of a new permanent watering point. Perhaps fortunately, the longer-term success of permanent water-point construction is often constrained by unsustainable technology. Almost invariably the power source that is to drive the pumping device required to lift the water to the ground surface (usually diesel pumps or windmills) runs into technical problems, usually related to maintenance.

A critical review of the history of pastoral development projects

Technology which may be appropriate in some circumstances can be rendered inappropriate or even dangerous by poor management. The experience of the paraveterinary programme in central Somalia which was implemented by the German bilateral agency GTZ, as a component of the larger Central Rangelands Development Project, highlights this point. The CRDP experience illustrates several areas where paravet programmes can go wrong. In this case, importation and distribution of drugs came under the control of the Somali Ministry of Livestock. Many drugs were withheld from sale by individuals within the Ministry, and a black market in the drugs developed at inflated prices. Black-market drugs were diluted to extend their value, creating the danger of a build-up of resistance to the drugs among target pathogens. The CRDP veterinary research programme discovered that tick-borne diseases in general posed no endemic restriction on animal production in the central rangelands.[41] However, because ticks were highly visible on the livestock, the pastoralists wrongly attributed a number of illnesses to their presence. Consequently the majority of drugs purchased and administered by pastoralists were tickicides (acaricides). Not only were pastoralists spending money on drugs which were unlikely to have any significant effect on animal disease levels, but the black-market custom of diluting drugs increased the likelihood that tick-borne pathogens would develop drug resistance. Consequently if tick-borne diseases became a major problem, the locally available drugs would probably prove ineffective.

Clearly the CRDP paraveterinary programme displayed some fundamental short-comings in its administration and design, not the least of which was a failure to utilise the veterinary auxiliaries as effective extension agents. As a result, much of the paravets' activities and drug sales were associated with tick control — at the very least an unproductive exercise, and at worst a serious limitation on the system's ability to confront any future outbreaks of tick-borne disease.

Another common feature of the technology associated with large projects is its complexity. The more complex the technology in general, the more difficult it is to transfer it to both beneficiaries and indigenous institutions. In addition, complex technology is more likely to have higher recurrent costs which must eventually be borne by either the host government or the beneficiaries. For these reasons, the introduction of complex technology is more likely to reduce the long-term sustainability of project activities once the donor or implementing agency has withdrawn.

Perhaps the most disturbing aspect of poor technology is that its introduction seems so often repeated in apparent, though inexcusable, ignorance of past mistakes. The choice of technology employed relates directly to the skills and training of the technicians designing and implementing the projects in question. Western-educated technicians are trained to address Western problems with Western solutions. Within the African pastoral environment the tendency to continue to define both the problem and its solution in these terms is therefore very strong, apparently even in the face of historical evidence which suggests otherwise.

Technicians with the flexibility, insight, and imagination to suggest technical solutions unique to the needs of African pastoralists have yet to emerge in any great numbers from the expatriate community — a fact which suggests that ultimately such people must be found from the ranks of indigenous technicians. Such technicians are most likely to gain the skills they require in local education systems specifically designed to address the needs of the particular country.

The omission of goals of justice and sustainability from the project design

The absence of goals concerned with social justice and sustainability from many project designs calls into question the fundamental philosophical basis upon which many interventions are made, and challenges evaluations of project 'success'.

Many NGOs have identified the need for social justice at the policy level, and make public claim to its incorporation at the project level. However, many of the larger multilateral and bilateral development agencies, although they have recently acknowledged the importance of 'social equity' goals, are accused of not implementing them effectively.

A review of the experience of pastoral development projects supports this observation. Larger projects specifically designed to address pastoralist poverty are almost non-existent within pastoralist Africa. Almost invariably, projects are designed to influence physical para-meters within the development environment. So the success of such projects is evaluated in terms of whether or not they have achieved these physical outcomes, rather than whether or not they have succeeded in achieving a fairer share of resources, or a stronger political voice, for the target group.

The importance of ensuring the longer-term sustainability of project initiatives has also received more attention in the development lit-

A critical review of the history of pastoral development projects

erature recently. Even if a project achieves the goals it set itself, the achievement is of little value if, once the external donor's technical and financial support terminates, so too do the project's activities. The practice of so-called *ex post* project evaluations is a relatively recent innovation within the development planning process. Even so, only one agency, the World Bank, claims to evaluate all of its projects, although most of the evaluations are undertaken only by its internal operational project staff.[42] Yet an evaluation carried out immediately after the external agency's responsibilities have ceased is of limited value. A more important question is: how well have the project activities survived and what impacts have they had five or ten years after the donor's departure? Such longer-term evaluations are extremely rare, yet it is this type of scrutiny which can really answer the question of how successful an intervention has been, and which would be more likely to reveal some of the fundamental lessons to be gleaned from development history.

For the larger donor agencies, livestock development projects within sub-Saharan Africa have resulted in the greatest concentration of failed projects in the whole world.[43] Yet even among the handful of projects that have been judged a success, this assessment was made merely on the achievement of the stated project goals. The above discussion calls into question the relevance of the goals themselves when they do not specifically include measures to address issues of social justice and sustainability.

External factors contributing to project failure

External factors are defined here as those factors whose origins are external to the immediate pastoral planning environment, but which nevertheless impinge upon it. The powerful influence which external factors can bring to bear upon the project environment stems from two inherent characteristics. Firstly, owing to their external origins, such factors are more likely to remain unrecognised within the local pastoral development planning process. Secondly, the externality (and often the scale) of these factors commonly renders them extremely difficult to accommodate or mitigate at the local planning level.

Two external factors can be identified which account for recurring project failures.

Unfavourable policy environments created by indigenous governments

When the larger development agencies carry out extensive investigations of the poor performance of their interventions in the African 'livestock sector', they almost invariably identify unfavourable indigenous-government policy environments as a major constraint on the achievement of their project and programme goals.

Adverse policy environments may relate to the livestock sector itself, or they may involve other sectors which in some way impinge upon the livestock sector. For example, government policies intended to sedentarise pastoralists through ranching schemes can change pastoralists' attitudes to land tenure, and thus may run counter to project initiatives intended to set up grazing reserves on public range. Government-imposed controls on meat prices, designed to provide cheap meat to growing and politically powerful urban populations, may limit the effectiveness of projects designed to increase market off-take of livestock by pastoralists.

Adverse policy environments can severely limit the effectiveness of project initiatives, yet it took considerable time for this fact to be recognised in the design and appraisal of projects. Most commonly adverse policy environments receive their first mention in *ex post* evaluations, in partial or total explanation of why the project in question did not achieve its objectives. This observation begs several questions. First, why do planners fail to recognise government policies antagonistic to project goals early on in the planning process? Second, what mechanisms are available to project planners to influence government policies?

Project planners commonly possess specific technical expertise, and consequently tend to concentrate on gathering data which relate to the narrow physical parameters to be addressed by the type of intervention planned. The potential impacts of government policies are for this reason often unrecognised in project design documents. In addition, government policies which might eventually affect the project's activities may ostensibly be operating in a sector other than the one being planned for. For example, government policies relating to the agricultural sector have on occasion had adverse impacts on the pastoral sector. Thus intersectoral relationships should be addressed as part of the planning process.

Faced with an adverse policy environment, project planners are confronted with four general options. They can try to modify government policy to make it more supportive of project goals; they can modify project goals in order to mitigate the impact of the adverse policy; they can proceed with the project and ignore the adverse policy environment; or they can abandon the intervention altogether.

The degree to which project planners can influence government policy will depend on a number of factors. The most notable of these are the support given to these policies from within the government relative to its support for the project; and the political decision-making power of the donor agency at the country, programme, and project levels. In general, agencies with sectoral programmes incorporating a number of projects have considerably more political influence than single-project agencies. This observation underlines one of the advantages of a programme approach to sectoral development problems.

Nevertheless, larger projects may be in a position to influence government policy at the project-design stage, though this influence is likely to diminish rapidly once the implementation stage starts. For this reason negotiations over modifications to government policy should take place early in the planning process, if they are to be successful.

Changing government policies to favour the achievement of project (or programme) goals may also have adverse impacts in sectors other than the one being planned for. Potential impacts on other sectors should be clearly identified and become part of policy discussions, which should focus on wider issues than those of specific interest to project planners.

The intrusion of implicit organisational goals of development agencies and governments

One important factor external to the local pastoral development planning environment is the existence of implicit organisational goals within both development agencies and governments. Many interventions suffer from a lack of recognition of these implicit organisational goals. Such goals may largely determine the type of intervention attempted, relatively independent of the nature of the problem being addressed.

An aid agency entering the field of development has a number of choices to make. Firstly it must choose the country and the sector in which it wishes to intervene. Then it must define the problem to be addressed, identify the target population who are to be the beneficiaries, and finally specify the nature of the intervention and set a time scale on the programme or project activities. The external agency must also decide whether or not to carry out the intervention in conjunction with an indigenous government agency or other group.

A critical review of the project experience discloses strong evidence to suggest that these 'choices' are often not choices at all. Within many agencies it would appear that so-called choices are in fact predetermined and formalised within the organisational structure. Essentially this means that a particular agency will define a certain development 'problem', identify target populations, specify the nature of the intervention, and define development goals, achievement timescales, and performance indicators, largely irrespective of the characteristics of the development environment in which it finds itself. This predetermined decision-making framework within which individual agencies address development issues will be signified in this and later discussions by the term *development style*.

The development style of a particular agency will be the net product of both its explicit and implicit organisational goals. The explicit organisational goals of an agency are those through which it publicly addresses a development issue. The implicit organisational goals are the unstated agendas which act to formulate development policy. Implicit organisational goals may be supportive of the explicit goals, or they may be antagonistic to them. Because implicit goals remain hidden, they are less easily identified and are therefore less likely to attract external criticism. For this reason they tend to be self-perpetuating, more enduring, and therefore (over the longer term) more powerful determinants of an agency's development style than its explicit goals.

For example, Morss and Honadle (1985), in reviewing the development project experience of the World Bank and USAID, conclude that development strategies and project designs tend to follow predetermined blueprints. They suggest that projects are designed to connote purposefulness and to exceed a minimum size, and observe that under these circumstances:

> The need to express certainty, largely dictated by the common goal of designing projects that will be approved, mocks the reality of conditions in developing countries. In these circumstances, it is not surprising that project design papers rarely offer useful directions for implementers. (Morss and Honadle 1985: 201)

The authors also conclude that among senior executives in donor agencies the goal of achieving financial-disbursement targets for recipient-country programmes receives higher priority than the manner in which the money is actually spent.

A recent review of the Australian overseas aid programme (Commonwealth of Australia 1984) identified goals implicit in the bilateral aid activities of the Australian Development Assistance Bureau (now known as the Australian International Development Assistance Bureau, or AIDAB). These included strategic, diplomatic, and economic goals designed to foster the interests of the donor country. Such goals can potentially influence all facets of the development planning process. This influence may begin with the initial selection of the country and sector in which the intervention is to take place, and extend to the definition of the problem to be addressed, the project design, the identification of the beneficiaries, and the selection of both the technology and the technicians who will implement it. These implicit goals have the potential to eclipse explicit goals to the extent that the interests of the donor agency (or donor country) exceed those of the recipients. Bilateral aid programmes are particularly susceptible to this conflict of interests. Implicit goals similar to those of AIDAB were, for example, identified for USAID.[44] Cassen (1986: 15), in a wide-ranging review of the development aid experience, concluded that

> On the donors' side, one of the most common causes of failure is the excessive intrusion of commercial or political motives.

While implicit goals are more likely to evolve into a powerful force within the complex bureaucracies of the larger aid agencies, they are not alone in this regard. Smaller NGOs which, for example, rely on the financial support of the public, are also susceptible to the influence of implicit goals. The need to foster public goodwill underlies a tendency for NGOs to amplify and publicise their project successes, while at the same time minimising exposure of their project failures. The danger in this tendency is that the lessons to be gleaned from failure may be buried under the wave of optimism.

An important source of implicit organisational goals are the development ideologies and the inherent values which drive them. While many NGOs with a humanistic development imperative publicly proclaim their development ideologies, others — particularly evangelical religious groups — do not. Nor is it common for government development agencies to do so. A number of international government agencies continue to base their development ideologies on unstated neo-classical economic beliefs. These beliefs, the notions of 'good' and 'bad' development they produce, and their concomitant assumptions regarding human behaviour and needs, directly influence development styles. Where values differ substantially between agencies, they act as severe impediments to development cooperation and the sharing of development goals and objectives between agencies. For example, in a number of fundamental ways belief systems based on neo-classical economic human behaviour conflict directly with those of humanistic origin. It is little wonder, therefore, that there has been a poor record of co-operation between certain types of government agency and certain types of NGO. With a few exceptions (for example Hoksbergen 1986), the literature has ignored the substantial issue of the belief systems that drive development ideologies. Worby (1988) makes the important point that government development policy often serves as a blueprint for political action. Development policy may therefore be largely a function of the prevailing political ideology, which in African countries may reflect the history of the emergence of the post-colonial state and the class interests that predominate within the state structure.

Development environments are complex arenas, and it is difficult enough to define appropriate and explicit goals for organisations and projects without the intrusion of powerful, unstated goals. However, by definition, implicit organisational goals are difficult to identify and discard. Their role in determining the nature and outcome of development interventions is rarely considered in project evaluations. Yet until organisations undertake substantive critical examinations of their implicit goals, such goals will continue to determine, both directly and indirectly, the nature of their development efforts. At least some of the repeated project failures within the African pastoral sector can be attributed to this lack of critical scrutiny of implicit organisational goals.

Conclusions

These twelve common shortcomings of pastoral development projects help to answer the question of why projects fail, but in doing so they raise other questions.

The first of these questions is why, with the apparent wisdom of hindsight afforded by project-evaluation documents,[45] are these shortcomings so frequently repeated with each subsequent project? The answer to this question relates in part to the inherent development style of aid agencies. Development styles and the philosophies underlying them tend to be entrenched within individual agencies. There is considerable resistance to change, even when it is vividly apparent that project success depends on fundamental changes in the goal orientation of the aid agency. With apparently unconscious irony, project documents often bemoan the unwillingness of pastoral groups to accept the behavioural changes demanded by agency-sponsored development initiatives. At the same time, the agencies themselves appear unwilling to make the behavioural changes demanded of them by both the development environment and project experience.

However, there would appear to be a more serious and fundamental flaw in the philosophy which underlies many pastoral development interventions. This is the assumption that pastoralists are trapped in a self-perpetuating, static environment of underdevelopment. The corollary of this assumption is that 'development' is primarily seen as entailing the transfer of technology to pastoralists — technology which will somehow improve their lot. In many respects it would appear that this assumption, and the intervention philosophies which result from it, are mistaken.

However, as recently as the last few decades many pastoral groups have been faced with profound modifications to their cultural environments. The problems besetting pastoral groups as a result are due not to ignorance or mismanagement, but to an inability to adapt quickly enough to these modifications to their world.

We will now examine in the Erigavo case study the nature and impacts of the forces of change upon one pastoral people, and the responses and experiences of one NGO, Oxfam (UK and Ireland), in trying to help these pastoral communities to adapt through development.

4

Case study: the Erigavo Erosion Control and Range Management Project

Introduction

The experience of the Erigavo Erosion Control and Range Management Project in North-West Somalia/Somaliland, funded and managed by Oxfam (UK and Ireland), on which the author was employed as co-ordinator between 1986 and the end of 1988, will enable us to explore a number of the issues raised in previous chapters.

We will examine a number of key questions about the project. What were the real causes of land degradation in the District? What evidence was there for recent forces of change operating within the area? What had been the behavioural responses of the pastoralists in the face of these changes? How should we define the development 'problem'? What was the NGO project experience, positive and negative, in seeking development strategies which attempted to meet the needs of the pastoral communities?

In this chapter we are concerned with defining the development problem within the Erigavo District — a critical first step. In the next chapter we will examine the Oxfam project's response to the development environment.

In examining the experience of the project, it is important to keep in mind the influences of political processes upon development. Here

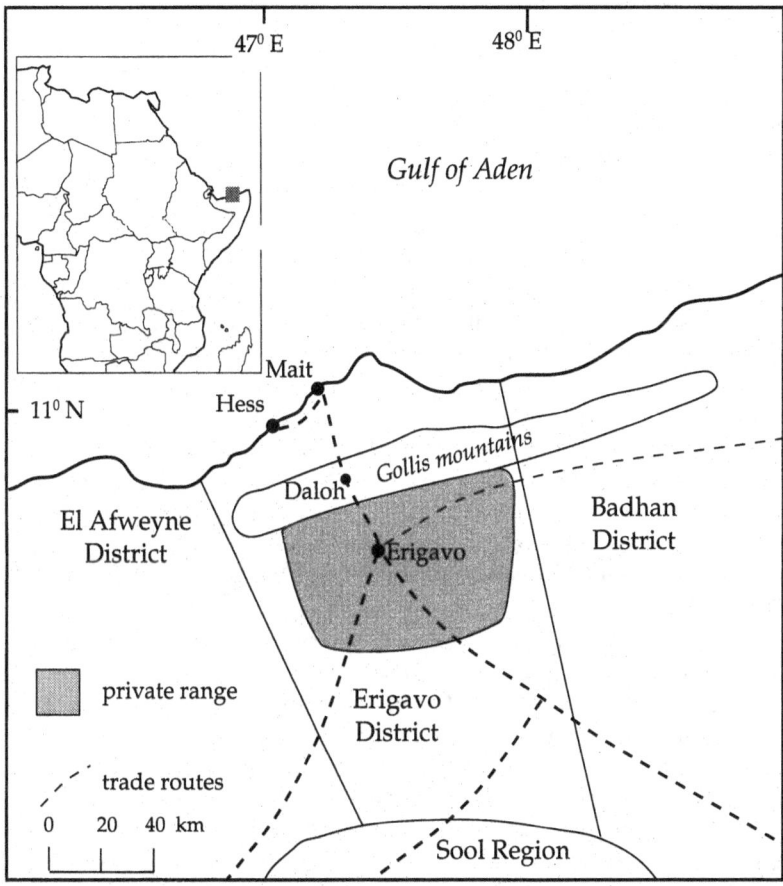

Figure 4.1: Erigavo District, Sanaag Region, North-West Somalia/Somaliland: towns and private range area

we are concerned with both macro-political and micro-political influences. Macro-political influences, such as the forces of change already discussed — regional and national insecurity, or government policy — are extremely important in terms of defining the development problem and the nature of appropriate interventions. Nevertheless the recognition and response to micro-political influences at the level of the project, or the community, can determine the success or failure of development efforts. As we shall see in the Erigavo example, pastoral development is often as much concerned with the management of conflict between competing interests as it is with physical or economic improvements.

Social causes of land degradation: the process of pastoralist settlement

The Erigavo District (Figure 4.1) is undergoing rapid land degradation. However, we must make a clear distinction between the immediate and highly visible physical causes and symptoms of this land degradation, and the rapid social, economic, and political changes operating both locally and nationally which constituted the *primary* causes of the land-degradation process.

The District was suffering from a loss of perennial grasses and thorny *Acacias* with a high grazing value, an increase in unpalatable weeds, and severe soil erosion. The rapidity of some of these processes of land degradation was highlighted by the fact that they had occurred within the lifetime of many of the pastoral elders.

The visible physical cause of land degradation was over-grazing, particularly by sheep and goats. Oral records suggested that much of the degradation had become evident within the last 20 years, a period that coincided with increased pastoralist settlement within the District. Much of this settlement entailed privatisation of public rangeland.

Officially, all rangeland belonged to the government, though the government was apparently uninterested in (and incapable of) exercising this control. Thus, before settlement and range privatisation took place, traditional systems of land tenure used to apply. These traditional systems of land tenure were flexible, depending upon circumstances. When food and water for livestock were in abundance, large tracts of the rangelands were generally considered open to all. However, the various clans traditionally maintained control over access to land next to their permanent home wells. During droughts, or during the later stages of the dry season, when supplies of feed and water were diminishing, the clans would fiercely protect the remaining grazing ground around their home wells. Conflicts over remaining water and grazing in the open-access range would also escalate at times of decreasing resources.

By 1988 approximately 3,000 square kilometres of formerly public range had been privately claimed. This settlement was mostly concentrated close to the township of Erigavo. An area of radius 40-50 km to the south of the town had been claimed as private range, as had the area to the north between the town and the edge of the mountain escarpment. (See Figure 4.2.) Private ownership of rangeland is illegal under Somali law (with the exception of ranch co-operatives), though ownership of agricultural land is legal.

The Erigavo Erosion Control and Range Management Project

Erigavo District, North-West Somalia/Somaliland: communal land on the high plains, denuded by over-grazing, which leads to rapid run-off of rainwater and consequent erosion.

Consequently the seizure of large areas of public rangeland by private interests within the Erigavo District received no offical recognition. This was despite the fact that considerable District and Regional resources were devoted to trying to resolve disputes which arose over the ownership of private rangelands. Moreover, at least one senior government official earned income from selling worthless and unsurveyed 'agricultural land titles' over parcels of range. Few pastoralists held even these titles, but merely claimed private rangeland by excluding others from using it. Needless to say, wealthier pastoralists managed to claim large tracts of better-quality grazing land, while poorer pastoralists claimed small areas which were little more than outcrops of rock.

The pastoralists who 'settled' generally did not maintain the majority of their livestock in permanent encampments. Rather they remained semi-nomads, moving away from their home areas in search of pasture for their animals when climatic conditions dictated. The process of settlement prompted two major behavioural changes among the pastoralists.

The first was a tendency to construct permanent dry-stone houses ('guri') on their privately claimed plots of rangeland, which replaced

Pastoral Development Planning

Erigavo District, North-West Somalia/Somaliland: a dummy stone house, constructed in order to lay private claim to once-communal rangeland.

their transportable animal-skin and woven-grass tents ('aqal'). These stone houses acted as a permanent reminder to other pastoralists that the particular area of range was now privately owned. Ownership was thus claimed, even though the house in question might remain uninhabited for periods of the year when livestock grazing was conducted away from the home area. Stone houses became so symbolic of land-ownership claims that some pastoralists constructed dwellings on desired range areas, thus laying claim to it and grazing their animals on it, without ever inhabiting the houses. These 'dummy' stone houses became more common as the process of range privatisation accelerated during the second half of the 1980s.

Secondly there was an increasing tendency to maintain the grazing sheep and goat flocks on the private range areas for longer periods than in the time before settlement took place. Some pastoralists would attempt to maintain a small grazing flock more or less permanently on the private range area. This practice was in part motivated by the need to maintain a presence on private range areas, in order to secure ownership against those who would claim it for themselves.

These two recent behavioural changes caused a major disruption to the traditional nomadic herding movements throughout the Erigavo

District. The traditional nomadic movements were based on the pastoralists' detailed understanding of the interactions between climate and the range ecosystem. Pastoralists moved to specific areas at specific times of the year in order to optimise their use of a particular type of vegetation. Thus at various times pastoral groups must move through the home areas of other pastoral groups in order to follow their traditional nomadic movements. In times of diminishing pasture or water for livestock, these periods of overlap have the potential for generating intense inter-tribal conflict.

The settlement and privatisation of public range on the plateau around Erigavo (the 'Ogo'; see Figure 4.2) severely disrupted the seasonal nomadic movements of the coastal ('Guban') pastoralists in particular. Where they had previously moved from the extremely hot coastal area over the escarpment and into the northern Ogo, their way was now barred by other pastoralists who laid claim to the rangeland upon which they would have formerly grazed or through which they would have formerly travelled. Consequently, traditional livestock movements have been blocked by this settlement and the animals now spend prolonged periods grazing the vegetation of the higher mountain areas. This has resulted in a rapid depletion of the vegetation in these high areas, leading to increased rainfall run-off and severe soil erosion on the lower plateau.

An additional source of grazing pressure was the rapid development of the ports of Mait and Hess as export centres for sheep and goats. As a result, increasing numbers of animals were herded and trucked through the Erigavo District. The grazing pressure, particularly in the coastal zone, increased markedly during the peak export periods. This was especially true of the areas immediately next to the ports themselves, as animals awaiting incoming boats grazed the ground bare.

Thus there is a strong causal link between the privatisation of rangeland and the recent acceleration of range-degradation processes. In order to address the problem of land degradation through development intervention, it is clear that there must be an understanding of the nature and causes of range privatisation.

The nature and causes of range privatisation in the Erigavo District

Spontaneous privatisation of land suitable for opportunistic rain-fed agriculture has been reported by Behnke (1987) for the agro-pastoral areas of central Somalia. Within the Erigavo District of the north, however, both agro-pastoral and purely grazing (range) land had undergone a recent period of rapid, spontaneous privatisation. This privatisation of range areas was therefore a unique phenomenon within the country. Land privatisation within central Somalia also involved land enclosure. That is, the land claimed would be clearly delineated and fenced off with thorn-bush (*Acacia*) fencing. However, within the Erigavo District there was a lack of thorn-bush material. Consequently the majority of the area claimed as private range remained unfenced and thus undemarcated in any visible manner. Travelling through this area, the casual observer would be unaware of any change in land tenure at all. The boundaries of individual private range areas were solely as perceived by the owners. Not surprisingly, disputes between neighbours over perceived boundaries were common.

Using the available evidence, we can speculate on the likely causes of the range-privatisation process as follows.

- The strict controls on land use enforced by the British colonial administration were not replaced with similar controls by the subsequent Somali administration after the British withdrew.

- During the 1970s a number of privately owned ranch co-operatives were set up by the national government, and were granted some of the best-quality grazing land within the District. From the viewpoint of the pastoralists, this constituted a government-sanctioned seizure of very productive range, effectively removing it from public use. The ranch co-operatives were resented by non-participating pastoral groups, who then began their own alternative and unofficial annexation of rangeland.

- Following the severe droughts and subsequent famines of the 1970s, the Somali government embarked on a policy of encouraging an increase in agricultural production within the country. One of the incentives for attaining this increase was that anyone cultivating and producing a crop on an area of land could retain that area in private ownership for as long as the agricultural production continued. One enterprising regional government official (now deceased) saw an opportunity to earn extra income, and began selling 'agricultural' titles, awarding ownership of range areas which were incapable of agricultural production. While private ownership of rangeland is ostensibly illegal under Somali law, this constraint was circumvented by classifying it as 'agricultural' land. Unfortunately no survey of the areas sold under title was ever conducted.

- The regional government gave policy support to the land-privatisation process, because it was felt that a trend towards settlement of the nomads was part of some form of 'civilising' process and would give pastoral people better access to facilities such as education and health care. Very importantly, it would be easier to impose and collect taxes from a more sedentary population — an imposition to which the nomads were notoriously resistant.

- The area within Erigavo District which had been privatised enjoyed certain advantages over other areas. These were the locally shallow water tables (which allowed the construction of a relatively high density of shallow hand-dug wells and allowed a higher density of grazing livestock to be supported); the proximity to the regional town of Erigavo and the animal-export markets; the high rainfall relative to other areas; and (before land degradation began) the relatively productive pastures.

Once initiated, range privatisation gained increasing momentum and fed upon itself. While many individual pastoralists claimed to harbour no personal desire to privatise range areas, they found themselves in a position where they apparently had no choice but to do so. Like a run on a bank, the allure of the rapidly diminishing resource was irresistible, and to ignore it would have been to fail to secure a parcel of land before all the remaining land was claimed by others.

The social costs and benefits of range privatisation

At least as significant as the environmental costs were the social costs of the changes in land tenure. The most visible social costs of the range-privatisation process were the frequent deaths of male pastoralists as a result of boundary disputes. However, the majority of social costs were borne by the pastoral women. Pastoral women are primarily responsible for the day-to-day management of the sheep and goat flocks. These animals constitute the largest livestock population within the District.

During 1987 and 1988 the Oxfam project conducted several surveys with the women of a number of pastoral and agro-pastoral communities. A technique of informal structured discussions was

Pastoral Development Planning

Erigavo District, North-West Somalia/Somaliland: counting sheep in a corral before they are released for the day's grazing. Women are primarily responsible for the day-to-day management of flocks.

adopted for the survey. Among other things, the women were asked to list the advantages (benefits) and disadvantages (costs) of the range-privatisation process.

The most frequently stated benefit of range privatisation was that the pastoralists no longer had to move away from their home areas with their livestock as much as they had done previously. That is, both the period and frequency of absence had diminished. Significantly, none of the women listed an increased access to educational and health facilities as being an advantage, in contrast to the beliefs of many regional government officials.

On the other side of the balance sheet, the pastoral women listed the costs of range privatisation as being:

- increased rates of soil erosion and vegetation loss, both within and outside the private range areas;
- increased difficulty in finding pasture for their livestock, particularly late in the 'Jilaal' (long dry season);
- the incidence of disputes over private range boundaries, in which

a number of women suffered heavy beatings by their neighbours;
- the increased difficulty and time involved in gaining access to watering points, owing to the need to circumnavigate the perceived (and commonly invisible) boundaries of the private range areas of others;
- an increased incidence of animal diseases (some of which they had never seen before), caused by the crowding of livestock and limited access to fresh pastures;
- the increased stress of having to continually and personally herd their flocks, to prevent them from crossing over their neighbours' unclear boundaries — a requirement which meant that the flocks could only rarely be left in the charge of the younger children, as had traditionally been done.

In addition to livestock management, pastoral women had the responsibilities of domestic production, as well as the education and raising of the children. Thus the extra stress and workload associated with their livestock management, which had been imposed as a result of range privatisation, was severely felt.

An additional social cost frequently referred to by the elders was the weakening of traditional kinship ties, which they claimed had occurred as a result of range privatisation. Some elders felt that, because individual family units were laying claim to their own private range areas, the traditional extended family was coming under threat. As evidence of this trend, the elders pointed to the fact that boundary disputes and associated killings often involved individuals who were quite closely related. They claimed that, while inter-tribal conflicts were traditionally common, serious disputes between close relatives were previously quite rare. In addition, the elders felt that their traditional decision-making power over social and land-use matters was being eroded, both by the emergence of 'nuclear families' on private rangeland and by the increasing imposition of government decisions and structures upon them.

On balance, therefore, the perceived social costs associated with range privatisation considerably outweighed the perceived social benefits. This view was generally held by male and female pastoralists alike. By 1988 regional government, on the other hand, had developed a somewhat ambivalent attitude to the relative social merits of the process. While still supporting the settlement of the nomads as being desirable in principle, the government was beginning to concede that the social costs were extreme.

The economic costs and benefits of range privatisation

The major benefits associated with range privatisation were economic. With increasing periods of settlement, the pastoral groups of the Erigavo District were being progressively dragged into the Somali equivalent of the modern market economy, and some benefited more than others. The lucrative livestock markets of the Arab Gulf states were becoming more freely available to the livestock merchants of the Erigavo District. The installation of a radio telephone in the town of Erigavo meant that the merchants could make daily contact with their agents in the Gulf, to determine market prices and forge deals. While the Somali live-animal export trade had suffered somewhat in recent years, owing to competition from Australian sheep in particular, Somali merchants had several advantages. First, they could respond to market fluctuations with reasonable speed. The sea transport of animals by *dhow* was cheap and reasonably fast (although risky, because animal losses due to poor handling were generally high, and the unseaworthy *dhows* would sink relatively often). With range privatisation and semi-settlement, the merchants now had a larger pool of animals from which to choose for export.

While some of the wealthier pastoralists use the fodder stored on their private range areas to fatten export-quality animals, most pastoralists do not specifically prepare animals for export or local sale, but merely dispose of them if and when they require the cash. Thus their livestock-husbandry goals are still far removed from what might be termed market production.

The development of a cash economy, coupled with the remittances from the Gulf in terms of goods-in-kind for the animals sold there, has meant that the average pastoralist now has greater access to consumer items such as mass-produced cooking utensils and clothing. Also now more readily available are substitute foods, in particular white flour and white rice. The pastoral women claimed that to a large extent these new foods were substituted for their traditional diet, based on meat and sorghum. This change in customary diet, while convenient for the pastoralists as the new foods can be easily stored and transported, had a negative nutritional impact. The new foods are significantly lower in iron and the B vitamins than the traditional meat and sorghum diet, and have been a major contributor to the high levels of maternal anaemia and maternal mortality evident in the District (Selden 1986). The Erigavo District has the dubious distinction of recording one of the highest maternal mortality rates in the world, a trend which could be markedly reversed if a return to the traditional diet could be achieved.

While the women physically managed the sheep and goat herds, decisions about selling livestock were normally made by the men. Men also maintained control of the money earned from the sales. The decision on whether or not to sell livestock was normally based either on an immediate need for cash, because pasture was diminishing and animals might die if not sold, or because merchants came into the areas seeking animals and offering high prices for them. This usually coincided with a strong export market.

In general, pastoralists did not use formal banking facilities such as that provided by the Central Bank in Erigavo. Some pastoralists did, however, employ an informal banking or credit system, using local town merchants, usually people to whom they were related. Excess cash could be left with a merchant for safe keeping until needed. Alternatively, the cash could be used to pay for goods such as rice or flour which would not be supplied immediately, but at some later date when required. Thus available cash could be employed to guard against inflationary price increases, an important consideration within an economy such as that of Somalia.

The question of the economic stratification of pastoralists and its likely impacts on decision making deserves mention. From estimates of individual pastoralists' flock sizes, and the areas of private range or agro-pastoral land they owned, it was clear that some degree of economic stratification existed within all the communities with which the Oxfam project had dealings. Within each community there would be a few individuals who quite clearly enjoyed greater wealth than the rest. Those who were apparently very wealthy often had strong connections with the market, either because they acted as livestock merchants themselves, or because they had a financial interest in a family operation.

The significance of economic stratification on decision making about development is that poorer pastoralists are more vulnerable and during periods of stress have fewer options than wealthier pastoralists. The poorer ones also tended to own smaller areas of range, and those which were the least productive. This meant that they had the most to lose from range degradation and the least to gain from the process of range privatisation. Wealthy pastoralists own larger areas of the more productive range. Thus they were more likely to look favourably on the process of range privatisation, primarily because they owned the greater share of it. While throughout community discussions the majority of pastoralists strongly supported reversing the process of range privatisation, some (but not all) of the wealthy pastoralists strongly rejected the notion.

It is likely that the development of the market economy, though still in its early stages, was in part both the cause of, and the result of, a trend towards settlement and range privatisation. The development of a cash economy, and the production of animals for sale rather than for subsistence, represents a fundamental and serious change in the objectives and values of the pastoral groups of the Erigavo District.

Conclusions

This discussion began by examining the physical causes of the soil erosion and vegetation loss occurring within the study area, which were identified as being due to over-grazing, particularly by sheep and goat flocks. If the 'problem' was defined at this level, a typical project intervention might involve bulldozer-constructed erosion-control work; perhaps attempts at revegetation of the rangeland; an attempt to encourage (or force) the pastoralists to reduce the size of their flocks; the delineation of grazing reserves; and perhaps an attempt at setting up further ranch co-operatives.

Yet, as illustrated in the above discussion and Figure 4.3, the primary causes of the over-grazing were increased settlement and range privatisation, and disruptions to the traditional nomadic herding movements. Thus there were fundamental changes to land-tenure and grazing systems. It is clear that development interventions need to be aimed at this level in the causal chain. Any attempt to intervene further down the causal hierarchy, as suggested above, would probably result in ultimate failure, because the higher-order causal processes would still be operating.

Certain social costs have accrued to the Erigavo pastoralists, particularly the women, as a result of range privatisation (see Figure 4.3). In addition there is evidence to suggest that the traditional systems of social organisation may be under threat from a new order. Should the development problem be defined at this social level?

Because substitute foods became available, and because livestock began to acquire a greater commercial value than subsistence value, the nutritional intake of the pastoralists had suffered and a major problem with maternal mortality was emerging. Should this issue be considered as part of the problem definition?

The Erigavo Erosion Control and Range Management Project

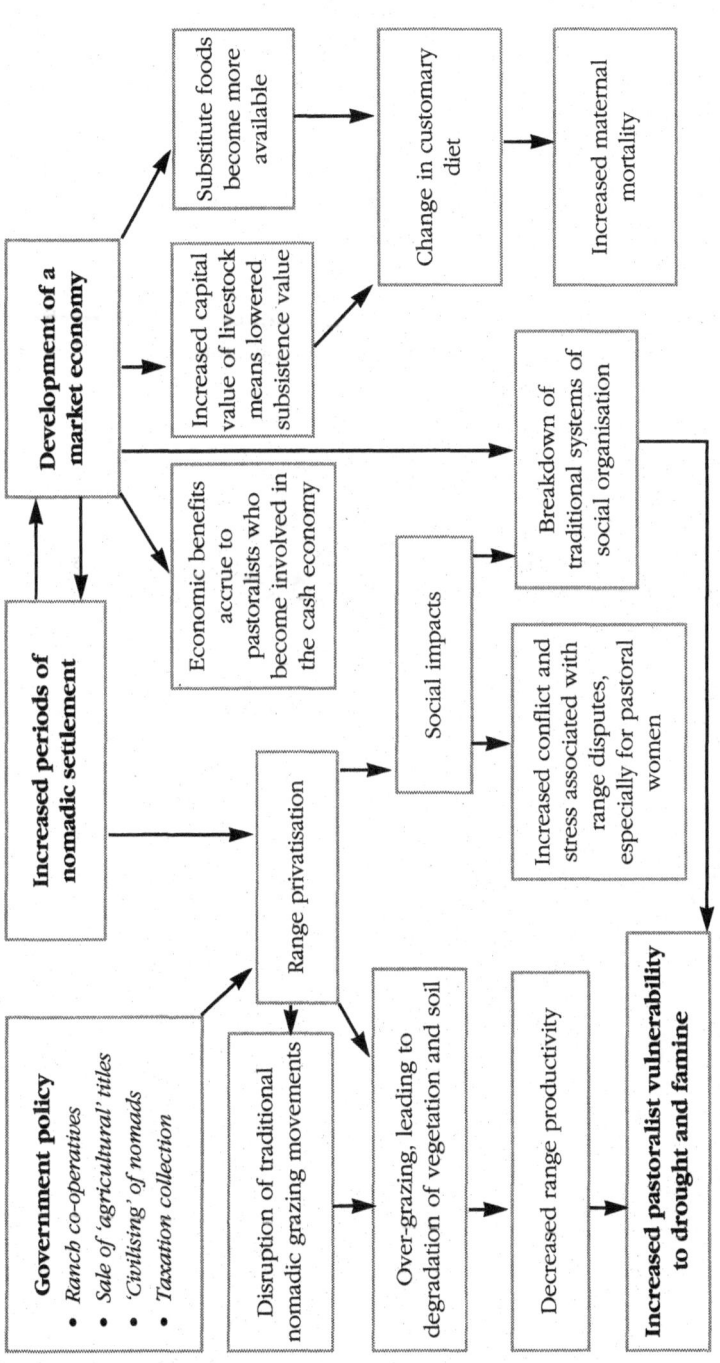

Figure 4.2: Problem definitions and causal linkages operating within the Erigavo District

Pastoral Development Planning

This brief discussion serves to illustrate three important points in relation to problem definition:

- Both vertical and horizontal causal linkages should first be identified, before any attempt at problem definition takes place.

- The problem should be defined, and interventions aimed, at the highest possible level in the causal chain.

- A problem can be defined in a number of dimensions, whether physical, economic, social, or political; failure to identify these horizontal links may largely explain the common occurrence of unplanned project impacts.

- Within the Erigavo District in the last 20 years, rapid environmental, social, economic, and political changes have been imposed on a culture and social systems which have developed over hundreds, if not thousands, of years. Thus in the broadest sense, the Erigavo District development problem may be defined in terms of an inability of the pastoral culture to adapt quickly enough to cope with these recent and rapid forces of change.

5

The development approach of the Erigavo Project

The project's development style

The 'development style' of an agency was defined earlier as being the net product of its explicit and implicit organisational goals. In practice, this means that package of strategies and values employed when choosing and designing a development intervention. Individual development agencies commonly employ a standardised and specific development style that is relatively independent of the problem being addressed.

Oxfam (UK and Ireland) funded and implemented the Erigavo Project. Oxfam's development style incorporated certain policies relating to the selection of beneficiaries, and the definition of problems determined the approach to the design, implementation, and evaluation of its projects. Project objectives and strategies, therefore, tended to adhere to certain loosely defined guidelines.

Oxfam saw its development role as being that of supporting self-help forms of community development. Its intervention rationale included the following policies.

- Sustainability of project activities, once the external funding and support had ceased, was considered to be of extreme importance.

- Interventions should be carried out at the level of 'communities', rather than that of individual contacts.

Pastoral Development Planning

- Benefiting groups should be selected on the basis of their relative poverty, on the basis of their vulnerability, or on the basis of their low social and political status. Within many development environments women, for example, would fall into this latter group.

- The communities should participate as much as possible in the design and implementation and ultimately in the evaluation of project activities. Projects should be seen to be addressing the expressed high-priority needs of the proposed beneficiaries.

- Interventions should involve low-cost, simple technologies which, if possible, should employ locally available skills and materials.

- Emphasis was placed on small-scale projects addressing the simpler problems, rather than on comprehensive intervention strategies.

- The *processes* by which development was achieved were given greater emphasis than the resultant forms of development. Consequently, only secondary importance was attributed to the achievement or measurement of quantitative results.

Two very important policies which did, however, underlie all Oxfam's development interventions were those of *flexibility* and *responsiveness*. It was recognised that in order to achieve a progressive understanding of the dynamic development environment, the project would need the freedom to respond to changing circumstances, unconstrained by fixed financial and development goals. Project objectives really did operate as 'hypotheses to be tested'.

Information-collection techniques: a learning-process approach

A major strength of the Erigavo Project was the manner in which it collected information and subsequently modified the nature of its development strategies. Faced with a complex development environment, the project required a philosophical foundation upon which to base its information-collection activities. Selected for this purpose was a strategy derived from the 'Learning Process Approach' as described by Korten (1980). In reviewing the common link between five successful development projects, Korten observed that essentially this approach involved:

The development approach of the Erigavo Project

... a learning process in which villagers and program personnel shared their knowledge and resources to create a program which achieved a fit between needs and capacities of the beneficiaries and those of the outsiders which were providing the assistance ... As progress was made in dealing with the problem of fit between beneficiary and program, attention was given either to building a supporting organisation around the requirements of the program, or to adapting the capabilities of an existing organisation to fit those requirements. Both program and organisation emerged out of a learning process *in which research and action were integrally linked*. (Korten 1980: 497; emphasis added)

The functional attraction of this form of development model is that data collection, project design, and implementation are viewed not as separate sequential steps, but as concurrent operations. Each activity is intimately interwoven in an incremental and iterative learning process. The learning process is viewed as being two-way, with both the project and the beneficiaries seeking and exchanging information.[1]

Data-collection techniques also took advantage of the project's physical strategies. The Erigavo District was characterised by two related degradation processes. The project was thus charged with two distinct yet interdependent activities. The first was to develop appropriate erosion-control techniques which would be adopted and constructed by the pastoral communities. The project's second task was to develop appropriate rangeland-management techniques which would limit the over-grazing which was contributing to the vegetation loss and soil erosion.

These two distinct activities proved to be highly suited to the learning-process approach. The learning process associated with the erosion-control activities developed relationships and encouraged understanding between the communities and the project. The trust engendered by this understanding created a firm foundation for the process of information collection and the progressive delineation of the behavioural choices available to the pastoralists in relation to rangeland management. For the pragmatic pastoralists, the erosion-control activities had the added advantage that the results were highly visible and the benefits immediately recognised. These activities also enabled the project to establish its credibility (a highly valuable and elusive commodity) with the communities.

Pastoral Development Planning

The project thus collected information in an incremental manner which was closely associated with both strategy definition and implementation. Four primary methods of information-collection were employed:

- structured group discussions;
- informal group discussions;
- individual interviews with key informants;
- participant observation.

Structured meetings were employed to direct group discussions to deal with specific information needs, issues, or problems associated with the project and community activities. Structured meetings were also an integral part of the delivery of a range-management education (extension) programme. This programme (employing colour slides from the local area, poster displays, and demonstrations) was designed to operate as both an educational package and a stimulus for discussion and the exchange of information.

Informal meetings were largely spontaneous and usually, though not always, occurred during the implementation of erosion-control works. Informal meetings were no less valuable than those more structured for the purposes of gathering information, but were of limited usefulness for problem-solving exercises.

Group meetings are an integral component of the pastoral Somali culture and are thus well suited to the uses outlined above. But Somali communities also lack the functional office of 'chief' common in the more settled communities of other cultures. At a group meeting all the 'elders' representing the community are given equal time to express their viewpoints. Women are almost entirely absent from such meetings, although an occasional exception is made for old women who have given birth to many male children. However, such women are rarely allowed to address meetings of elders. While young men may attend, they are generally not permitted to address the meeting until approaching middle age. Thus unless efforts are taken to correct this bias, data-collection based on traditional community meetings may be distorted to reflect solely the views (and the needs) of the older men. Thus both a potential gender-bias and an age-bias in information-collection had to be accounted for, and methods adopted to limit this bias. Once the project's credibility had been established within a particular community, it was then possible to start seeking the viewpoints of the women of that community through group meetings. Consequently it was possible (on the whole) to avoid gender-bias during data-collection and information-exchange sessions.

However, the issue of age-bias in data-collection and relationship-building was not originally recognised by the project. This oversight proved to be a significant factor within two communities in regard to the erosion-control activities. Once this was recognised, measures were introduced to improve contact with the younger men of each community, particularly during erosion-control training. The details of this issue will be outlined later in the discussion.

Individual interviews were conducted as appropriate with those key people (often non-pastoralists), such as government officials or livestock merchants, who could contribute the specialist information deemed necessary for the study.

The final technique used for data-collection was that of participant observation. In the context of the Erigavo study, participant observation proved to be by far the most valuable mechanism for data-collection. In particular, information relating to the *unstated* social and political processes occurring in the district was gathered using this method. Issues such as tribalism, the social and political relationships between and within communities, and the relationships between pastoral communities and government could not be addressed directly through community meetings or individual interviews. Somali pastoral groups are traditionally reluctant to reveal the nature of these relationships to those to whom they are not closely related. Reinforcing this taciturnity was pastoralists' fear of government reprisals if they were seen to be too open with Westerners. Yet an understanding of these political and social issues is critical to an identification of the various influences on pastoralists' decision-making processes, the non-physical causes of the rangeland-degradation processes affecting the District, and the range of politically and socially acceptable behavioural choices available to pastoral groups as coping strategies in the face of rapid change.

Casley and Kumar (1988: 41) define participant observation as being:

> a type of qualitative data-gathering method that requires direct observation of an activity, behaviour, relationship, phenomenon, network, or process in the field ... The participant observer seeks to go beyond outward appearances and probe the perceptions, motives, beliefs, values, and attitudes of the people involved.

Essentially the observer participates in the 'social reality' of the group under observation. Within the context of the semi-nomadic pastoral communities of the Erigavo District, full participation in their social reality was impossible for project staff. To fully participate one would have to be a pastoralist with kinship ties to the group under observation. Nevertheless, extended periods spent living with pastoral communities, working with them on erosion-control structures, and meeting with them meant that considerable insights were gained.

The major disadvantages of the participant-observer technique are, first, that it is time-consuming; second, it relies heavily upon the relative perceptiveness and observational skills of the individual observer; and third, care should be taken to exclude (as far as possible) the intrusion of the personal bias of the observer.

The advantages of the participant-observer technique lie in its ability to identify issues, perceptions, and processes which remain unstated by the community members. Such issues may remain unstated because the communities are either unwilling to enunciate them, or because they are incapable of enunciating them, or because they are unaware of them.

An additional advantage of the participant-observer technique within the context of this study is that it is well suited to the framework of the incremental learning-process approach. As the learning process proceeds, recognition and comprehension of social and political processes improves, non-indigenous workers' language skills develop, data-collection and implementation continue concurrently, time constraints are minimal, and the effectiveness of the participant observer gradually increases.

The relationship between the learning-process approach adopted by the Erigavo Project and data-collection, intervention-design, and implementation is illustrated schematically in Figure 5.1.

The erosion-control component: whose definition of development?

The project's erosion-control activities involved a community-development exercise designed to educate and train community members about the causes of, and solutions to, erosion processes. These activities had technical, social, and political components to them.

Over a two-year period the project trained representatives from 15 agricultural, agro-pastoral, and pastoral communities with a total population of around 2,500 people. The majority of the training took

The development approach of the Erigavo Project

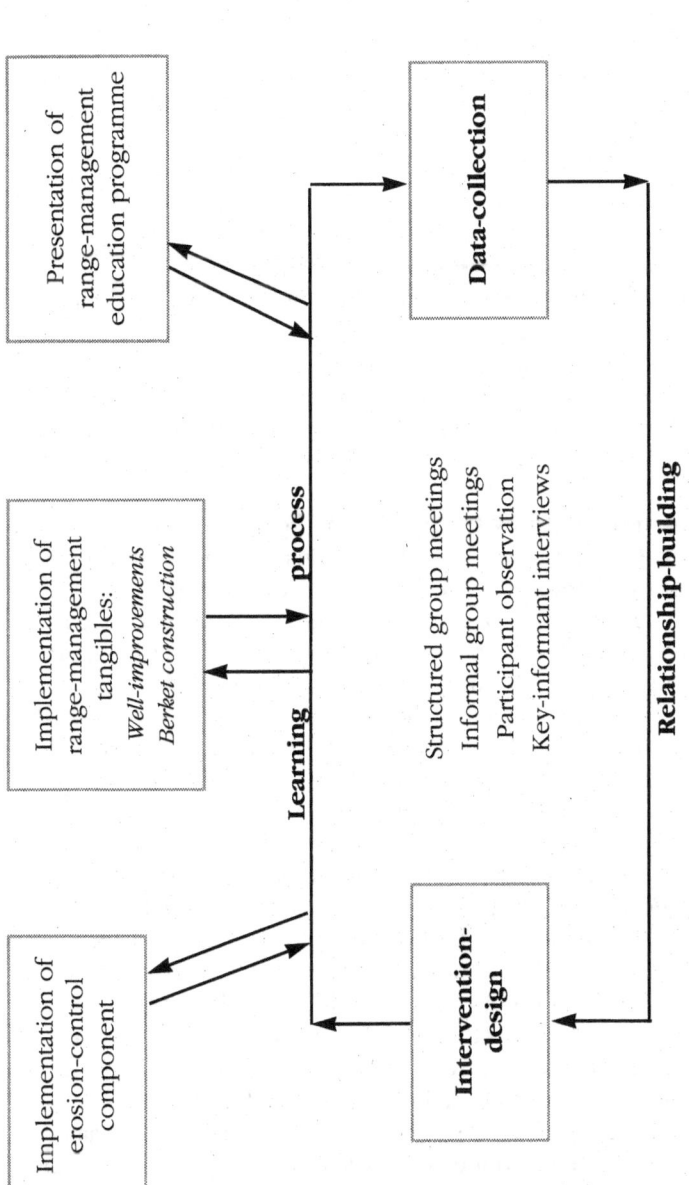

Figure 5.1: Schematic representation of the 'learning process' approach adopted by the Erigavo Project, and its relationship with data-collection, intervention-design, and implementation

place in the second twelve months. The first twelve months involved the incremental development of an appropriate community-development model through initially working with just a few communities. Mistakes were made, but, because of the incremental development style, they were small rather than large mistakes. Information-gathering and the development of the technical and development skills of the project staff were also given critical attention during the first twelve months.

Initially there was a considerable gap between how the communities defined the problem and its solutions and the manner in which the project defined them. The communities viewed their erosion problem as the large gullies (many more than five metres deep) which were forming up the centre of their farming or grazing areas. Their proposed solution to this problem involved Oxfam using bulldozers to control these gullies for them. Because of its particular development style, Oxfam defined the problem and its solutions differently.

The Oxfam project saw the problem as being primarily that of the inappropriate use of land (which explains the range-management component of the project). The project viewed erosion-control works and education as only a part of the solution. Staff judged bulldozer-constructed works to be unsustainable, and argued that community-constructed rock bunds and manually applied gully-stabilisation structures would be preferable. In addition, the project decided that the cost and feasibility of filling in the large gullies were questionable. Rather the project advised the communities to direct their resources towards building bunds, and controlling the smaller gullies which, if left uncontrolled, would also increase in size.

Thus the goals of sustainability and simple low-cost technologies were judged by the project to be of higher priority than that of allowing the community to define entirely the problems and solutions. Clearly, the policies which together constituted the development style of Oxfam were not all compatible in this instance. Consequently the project's first role was not so much one of implementing erosion-control structures, but one of helping the communities to understand Oxfam's definition of development.

The second constraint on the introduction of Oxfam's definition of development was the requirement that the project's activities should be based on the community-development model. 'Communities' within this model may be defined as groups of individuals or families who are reasonably close (in a geographical sense) to one another,

The development approach of the Erigavo Project

Somalia: erosion made worse by FAO-funded attempts to control it. Poor engineering caused the collapse of the 'gabion' wall (top); and diverted flood waters created a new gully (bottom)

and who have some form of group consciousness and history of group co-operation. However, this concept of 'community' could not be neatly applied to the Erigavo District pastoralists.

An identification of the local frameworks of social organisation would be critical to an understanding of pastoralists' decision making and for the formulation and implementation of development initiatives. Thus the Oxfam project gave particular attention to understanding these local social frameworks. The Erigavo District pastoralists belonged to four broad clans: the Dulbahante, Warsengeli, Habar Yunis, and Habar Jaalo. Inter-clan conflicts were common, especially during times of climatic or political stress. While these clans were the basis for broad allegiances, they nevertheless constituted too broad a level of kinship to be relevant to local-level decisions about land use and development. Also, the Somali government had ostensibly declared 'tribalism' illegal, which meant that there could be no public discussion of clan allegiances. However, community discussions and interviews with key informants led to the delineation of three levels of indigenous social organisation which would be relevant to pastoral development activities. These were:

- The close kinship level of 'dia-paying' groups, which did not necessarily live close together. ('Dia' literally means 'blood', and a dia-paying group is a more closely related, and contractually bound, sub-set of the clan.)

- The concept of 'community' based on geographic proximity, which generally involved members from the same tribe (i.e. clan), but which might, on occasion, contain members of the same dia-paying group, or members of other tribes. Communities were commonly associated with sub-catchments or valleys, particularly in the agro-pastoral and agricultural areas.

- The broader geographic concept of *beel*, which incorporated all the various communities, and therefore tribal groups, who traditionally used a major well or group of wells.

The concepts of 'community' and *beel* represent relatively recent, non-tribal levels of social organisation. They were cultural responses to the process of pastoralist settlement where changing social relationships were required to accommodate new forms of social contract and co-operation.

None of these levels of social organisation closely approximated to the Oxfam community-development model. Traditionally, the only

The development approach of the Erigavo Project

level at which the Somalis had demonstrated group co-operation was within the kinship contract of the 'dia-paying' group, a sub-set of their clan family. However, dia-paying groups could not be utilised by the project for two reasons. Officially their existence was illegal (at least they were as far as the project's operations were concerned), and members of the same dia-paying group would not necessarily live near to one another.

Thus for the erosion-control component the project had no choice but to work initially with those groups which were geographically close to each other and which were often, but not always, members of the same clan. The limitations which this condition placed on the implementation of the community-development model were that these 'communities' usually had no history of group co-operation, while on the other hand they often had a history of conflict over the rights to land. In addition, where several clans were present, they resisted the suggestion that they should work together. Thus communities were geographical groupings of individual households which might or might not have had kinship ties with one another.

Nevertheless, the scale of the erosion problem and the low population densities meant that group implementation of erosion-control works was necessary. Thus the major task of the project was not so much to train communities in erosion-control techniques, but to strengthen over time the organisational and consensus-seeking strength of these communities.

However, as its learning process progressed, the Oxfam project worked with the level of social organisation that was appropriate for the development issues being addressed. Thus when extending and implementing erosion-control techniques, the project worked at the community level. When involved with improvements to wells, the project deal at the level of *beels*. On range-management extension the project initially worked at the community level. However, because of the social and physical complexity of range-management issues, and because of the scale of strategies that would be required in order to address the problems evident in the District, dealing at the community level was obviously not enough. Ultimately the project would have to work at the level of *beels*, or groups of *beels*, if it was to have any impact on changing behavioural patterns.

Erosion-control: community-development strategies

The erosion-control works were undertaken with the men. The project staff judged that the existing heavy workload of the pastoral women in relation to domestic production and small-livestock husbandry meant that they would be incapable of meeting this additional imposition. While not carrying out physical works, the women were involved with the erosion-control and range-management education programme which was presented to them by the project's Women's Development Officer.

The project began working with one agricultural community, selected because it was one of the most settled of all the communities within the District. It had also previously demonstrated the ability of its members to work together, albeit in a limited form.. Initial contact with the agricultural community allowed the project to refine both the technical aspects of its work and the organisational aspects. As the project moved away from the agricultural community to work increasingly with the more conflict-prone and organisationally weak agro-pastoral and pastoral communities, new difficulties emerged which had to be addressed.

The pattern of working with communities on erosion-control works evolved over a period of almost two years. In the early stages of this evolution many mistakes were made, most of them recognised and, if so, generally not repeated. Significantly, the project understood that each community had to be treated as a unique entity. It had its own history, its own experience or lack of experience of community decision-making, conflicts, personalities, goals and needs, and finally its own definition of the problem and its solutions. The ease and speed with which an individual community adopted the project's model of community development largely depended upon its inherent organisational strength. This in turn depended upon its history of group action. In general, most of the communities with whom the project was dealing had no experience of implementing community works.

The usual sequence of dealing with a community was as follows. Project staff and community representatives would meet and discuss at some length the nature of their erosion problems (and other matters), and the manner in which the project worked with communities such as theirs. Considerable time was devoted to explaining to the communities the concepts entailed within Oxfam's definition of development. Project staff explained in detail what was expected from the community in terms of its contribution to the works, and what contribution would be provided by the project. This initial contact and explanation were of

The development approach of the Erigavo Project

critical importance, because conflicts could so easily result from the community's incomplete understanding of these respective roles. An inspection of the whole community area and its erosion problems was then undertaken in conjunction with the local elders. The community was then asked to organise itself and, through a series of community meetings, to select a keeper of the tools required for erosion-control works. Also selected would be a group of trainees (usually 10-15 per community). The trainees were instructed in the erosion-control methodology and were expected to spread their new knowledge eventually throughout the rest of the community. The project played no part in the selection of the tool keeper or trainees.

The community trainees were trained in a small range of erosion-control techniques. The initial training would usually involve the stabilisation of a moderate-sized gully (up to two metres deep) and the construction of a number of stone contour-bunds. This training was normally carried out over two or more days and included an evening slide show and discussion session. These evening sessions had the dual objective of undertaking erosion-control extension and providing an opportunity to gather further information on pastoralists'

Erigavo District, North-West Somalia/Somaliland: members of a Caduur agropastoralist community working on an Oxfam-funded gully-stabilisation scheme. The gully threatened to engulf a small farm nearby.

83

decision-making processes. This additional information later contributed to the development of the rangeland-management education programme, and to the identification of potential range-management strategies for the District.

Oxfam supplied the tools required to undertake the works, and a truck for the transport of the necessary stones. The tools (shovels, pick axes, wheelbarrows, hoes, etc.) were supplied to the communities on loan. This loan was originally intended to be nominal. However, the fact that the tools remained the property of the project in the eyes of the community proved to be critical during the early stages of the development of the organisational skills of a number of communities.

After the initial training, it was left to the community to decide on the sites for future works (taking technical advice from the project staff), and the timing of those works. Communities normally attempted works of progressively increasing difficulty. 'Advanced' communities were experimenting with diversions of rainwater from 'tugs' (drainage lines carrying spate flows) for the opportunistic irrigation of their pastoral and agro-pastoral areas.

More critical than the development of technical skills, however, was the progressive development of the organisational skills of each community. Initially a community might take months to select its trainees and choose work sites, and during this period might require several supporting visits from the project. After twelve months of contact, some communities could organise themselves and their labour and choose their erosion-control sites. All that was subsequently required from the project was a one-day visit to provide technical advice on the proposed works. The community would indicate for how long it required the truck for transporting rocks, and would implement the works with no further input from the project.

While some of the communities managed this smooth progression to group decision-making and group action, other communities negotiated a more tortuous route. In such instances the project had to manipulate its inherent political power in order to achieve its community-development goals.

The project's role as a political instrument

The neat model of community development described above in fact applied to perhaps only ten per cent of the communities with whom the project had contact. For most communities it was their first contact with 'development', and thus their first contact with external

The development approach of the Erigavo Project

offers of aid and resources. At some stage during the development process many communities split through disagreement. Rather than acting as a mechanism for group decision-making and group action, the project initially acted as a catalyst for conflict. Usually these conflicts would emerge after the project and the community had undertaken the initial erosion-control training and the community was left to its own devices to set its work priorities and start working together in the absence of the project.

Often the project had difficulty identifying the existence and nature of the conflict. Somali culture holds that internal conflicts must not be displayed to outsiders. Thus a community might be riven by an internal dispute for several months before the project became aware that a conflict existed. The project would then have to institute a series of community meetings before it became aware of the nature and cause of the conflict. Even after going through this exercise, the staff would sometimes still not be sure of the causes of the conflict.

There were a number of sources of conflict. The two most commonly recurring related to the possession of the erosion-control tools, and disagreements between the younger male members of the community and the elders. While communities were asked to choose the keeper of the tools themselves, they often disagreed over this choice at a later date. The tool keeper was viewed by community members (and by some tool keepers) as being in a position of implicit power. Sometimes the tool keeper was seen as representing one faction or another within the community, and thus the faction that he did not represent would argue that their representative was a more suitable tool keeper. On other occasions the tool keeper would refuse to lend tools to those he did not like or to whom he was not related.

Other sources of conflict were disagreements between the young men of the communities and their elders. These disagreements were able to escalate within a few communities because of the earlier failure of the project study to recognise the age-bias in its method of information-collection. During the early stages of collecting information, the project was compelled by cultural protocol to be seen to be dealing in the first instance with the community elders. In order to contact the women, the project was obliged initially to obtain the permission of the elders. While it was expected that gender-determined differences would be encountered in relation to the needs of the pastoralists, age-related differences were not foreseen. During the initial data-collection it was assumed that the decision-making processes, and in particular the goals and needs, of the younger and older pastoralists were more or less similar. This proved to be incorrect. The elders had greater political power in relation to community decision-making than the young men. The young men had young families with dependent children and were still building up their flocks. They were in general more economically and environmentally vulnerable than the older men. Thus while the elders could afford extensive delays in their erosion-control works as a result of disputes, the younger men felt that they could not. In addition, the elders were more likely to have built up individual antagonisms within their communities over time, and were also more likely to become involved in political power-struggles.

The project was thus faced with a dilemma in such communities. The elders held most of the political decision-making power. In order to work within a community the project had initially to deal with the powerful elites, that is the elders, in accordance with cultural protocol. Failure to observe this protocol by, for example, marching in to a community and organising a meeting between the project and women's groups would have guaranteed instant exclusion. To work effectively with a community, the project then had to establish a relationship of trust, not only with the elders, but also eventually with the sub-sets of each community with whom it wished to deal, such as the young men and the women. In those communities where the elders were less inclined towards political power-games, this relationship developed relatively easily. In order to influence the decision-making in those communities racked by internal dissension, the project, with its repertoire of skills and resources, employed a package of strategies. Project staff adopted three primary strategies: making direct comparisons with other communities; acting as a mediator/negotiator between conflicting groups; and retrieving the erosion-control tools.

An effective method of encouraging a community to reach agreement was to take the elders on a tour of another community far more advanced in its group decision-making and implementation of soil and water conservation works. These works had the advantage of demonstrating immediate and highly visible benefits. This was particularly true of water conservation for increased crop and pasture production, and the visitors would usually depart extremely impressed. This exercise was more effective if the two communities were of different tribes. Thus the visiting elders could judge the benefits which were accruing to the other community — but not to

The development approach of the Erigavo Project

themselves, because of their internal dissension. This simple exercise worked in most cases of low-level conflict, and normally the community would soon afterwards find within itself the means for reaching agreement.

Where conflicts were intense, and where conflicting groups and the nature of the conflict could both be identified, the project acted as a mediator or negotiator between these groups. Sometimes these conflicts would be resolved through negotiation. On other occasions the only alternative was for the community, in its dealings with the project, to sub-divide along the lines of the warring factions.

Within communities where either the conflicting groups or the nature of the conflict could not be identified, the project usually chose to retrieve the erosion-control tools. Originally the tools were never intended to return to the project's possession and were only nominally on loan to the community. That they were seen by the community as being on loan allowed this action to be taken. However, communities who had their tools removed from their possession were never allowed to feel that this action constituted some form of punishment. The project offered a consistent reason for retrieval of the tools. This was that the tools were in limited supply. As the community in question was not constructing erosion-control works and obviously had no need of them, the project required the tools for another community who urgently wished to start their works. Commonly, communities would soon find within themselves the organisational skills required to agree to recommence work, and would subsequently approach the project for a renewal of the tools loan.

Once the project had worked successfully with a number of communities, it began to establish its credibility within the District. This credibility extended not only to the project's technical attributes and its ability to deliver tangible benefits. Its credibility also reflected its apparent independence both from government (which was strongly mistrusted by pastoral communities) and from tribal issues. As this credibility increased, so too did the project's ability to contact and work with sub-sets within the community such as the young men and later (in relation to range management) the women. Within two communities the young men became so frustrated with the inability of their elders to agree to work together that they approached the project to work with them independently of their bickering elders. In the early days of its activities the project would have been unable to take this action, as the elders would have maintained the power, if they wished, to exclude the project. However after 18 months of intense activity within the District, staff were in a position to start work, somewhat cautiously, with the young men alone. Within both these communities the sight of the young men working to overcome their erosion problem prompted the elders eventually to begin their own works. The project, through its own political decision-making power, was having an influence on the decision-making balance within the communities.

This account illustrates four important issues which are likely to emerge with any project seeking participatory development at the community level.

- The project was operating simultaneously at two levels: the physical level of erosion control, and the socio-political level. The project thus operated as a participant in changing socio-political community relationships.

- The term 'community participation' covers a whole range of decision-making power balances between a project and the beneficiaries. The project, in imposing its own model of development, found itself initially in a position of control. Over time, as a community developed its organisational skills, the development environment progressively moved to one of partnership between the project and the participating communities. Finally, as the communities took on more responsibility for the organisation and implementation of soil and water conservation works, they were increasingly in a position of control over development activities. Thus beneficiary participation proved to be an evolutionary process, the rate of evolution varying markedly between communities. This relationship is illustrated in Figure 5.2.

- In order to encourage this evolutionary process, the project at times had to intervene as a political entity. Thus to implement its definition of development, the project had to diverge considerably from what might be described as the simple conventional model of participation. This model assumes a uniformity among community members both in terms of their expressed needs and in terms of their ability to participate. Within the project's erosion-control activities, the process of participation was as much a process of negotiation between strategic groups, of which the project was only one faction. The importance of the project in this equation is that it had the political power to encourage the negotiating processes that enabled

The development approach of the Erigavo Project

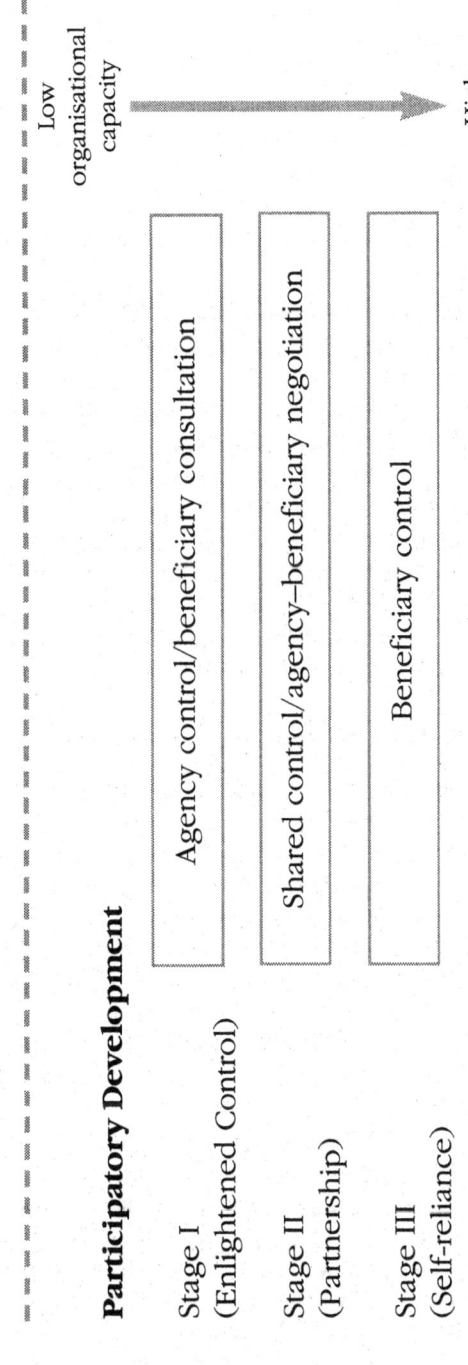

Figure 5.2: Participatory development as an evolutionary process

the needs of the less powerful groups to be met. Thus a project can be employed as an instrument of political change. This change may bear little relationship to the technical interventions being made. More significantly, the change can involve modifications to the decision-making environment, so that the balance of power may be shifted from one group to another. In initiating these modifications a development agency must be aware of their eventual impacts, both desirable and undesirable, upon the communities with whom it is dealing.

- The strengthening of the organisational capabilities of some communities was very time-consuming. While a few communities were capable of working effectively in the absence of the project after only a few months, others were still requiring support almost two years after first contact. The flexibility of Oxfam's development style allowed these unpredictably long lead times to be incorporated into the implementation time-scale. There were no quantitatively defined performance indicators to which the project had to adhere. Each community could be treated as a unique entity. If an individual community was unable to work with the project at the predetermined time, the project would simply reschedule the planned works and move on to the next community on the list.

Project monitoring: objectives and procedures

Monitoring activities were deliberately maintained as simple, informal, continuous procedures, as opposed to the more complex and therefore discontinuous monitoring procedures which are often adopted on larger projects. Monitoring was viewed as an integral component of project implementation which provided feedback information to allow on-going responsive modifications to project design. Monitoring activities fell into two categories. The first involved the monitoring of the physical or technical progress of the implementation of soil and water conservation works. The second involved the monitoring of the social and political components of the development process.

Monitoring of the physical and technical progress of implementation primarily involved checking that works were constructed in such a way that they would fulfil the function expected of them, that works damaged by flooding were being repaired by the communities, and that the communities were maintaining their enthusiasm for the on-going implementation of works.

The development approach of the Erigavo Project

Monitoring of the social and political components of the development process proved to be the most critical factor in the success of the project. The building up of a community's ability to take decisions as a group, its organisational capacity, and its self-reliance were important project goals. The development style adopted by the project also determined that the achievement of these non-material goals was a fundamental prerequisite if the more tangible goal of implementing SWC structures was to be achieved. In monitoring the social and political components of the development process, the project largely found itself involved in the processes of conflict-management and negotiation, as described previously. As an actor in the development process the project, through either its actions or its mere presence, often became both source of and witness to the conflict. The monitoring process achieved several purposes in relation to conflict management.

Firstly, intense monitoring of progress in community development was possible, owing to the limited number of communities with whom the project would be involved at any one time. Consequently, when conflicts emerged, they would normally be identified early on in the process. The longer that conflict remains unrecognised and uncontrolled, the more it is likely to intensify, and eventually the more difficult it will be to resolve.

Monitoring of project activities was also concerned with the issue of community participation in the development process. Specifically, the project was concerned with the issue of whether the less wealthy or less powerful within each community had access to the decision-making process and the implementation of erosion-control works on their land. In monitoring the achievement of this development objective, the project was aided in this task by the Somali custom of deciding on important issues through the medium of a large public meeting. All were invited to these meetings and, in theory, all were entitled to express their points of view. Thus community decision-making was a very public affair in which all viewpoints had the chance to be aired. In reality the women virtually never addressed such a meeting, and the young men rarely. The inability of both women and young men to participate to the same degree as the older men meant that ultimately these two groups had to be dealt with separately.

An evaluation of the erosion-control activities

As the Erigavo Project was prematurely terminated in early 1989, with the outbreak of the Somali civil war, no *ex-post* evaluation was ever carried out. Thus to evaluate the progress of the project's activities, this study must rely on assessments made as part of the on-going monitoring procedures. The erosion-control component of the project's activities may be evaluated at three levels:

- the appropriateness of the project's explicit and implicit objectives (that is, its development style);
- the degree to which these objectives were achieved, and the impacts (both planned and unplanned) of these activities on the development environment;
- the broader implications of this project experience for similar projects elsewhere.

Two key elements of the project's development style appropriate to the Erigavo development environment were those of flexibility and responsiveness. Financial flexibility allowed available funds to be redirected towards alternative activities in response to priorities that shifted over time. As the technical strategies to be adopted were not resolutely defined at the outset, responsive and appropriate strategies could be progressively derived. Thus financial and technical flexibility allowed the project to respond more effectively to the progressive learning process of development.

The components of the project's development style which deserve examination are its emphases on participatory development and the development of self-reliance and organisational capacity. Ultimately these three interrelated processes would determine the eventual sustainability of the project's activities.

There was a distinct change in the nature of community participation as activities progressed from those of erosion control to those of rangeland management and questions of land use. Within the erosion-control activities, community participation was an important requirement to ensure the on-going sustainability of the implementation of soil and water conservation works. Thus participation was viewed primarily as a strategy for achieving the objective of sustainability. Within the rangeland-management component, development issues were directly related to the quality and form of the future lifestyle of the pastoralists involved. Thus community participation became an ideological as well as a practical necessity. That is, the rights of the pastoralists themselves to make crucial choices regarding their future became important. Consequently, rather than acting as a strategy for the achievement of other objectives, community participation became a clear and primary development objective in its own right.

The development approach of the Erigavo Project

It is important to distinguish between the concepts of beneficiary *participation* in the development process, and that of *control* of the development process. Within the project's erosion-control activities the co-operating communities participated in the decision-making at every stage of the process. Firstly they chose whether to be involved in the project's activities. Subsequently they chose their trainees and tool keepers, and the dates, locations, and frequency of soil and water conservation works. Initially, however, the project imposed its model of development upon the co-operating communities, and maintained control of the implementation methodology. Even the 'proximity' concept of community adopted by the project, while recognised by the pastoralists, was loosely defined when compared with their 'kinship tie' concept of co-operative behaviour. As an individual community improved its organisational capacity and technical skills, it took on greater control of its erosion-control activities. Once confident of their abilities, individual communities would devise their own appropriate implementation methodology. Some communities maintained their whole-community involvement in each soil and water conservation construction, as originally recommended by the project. Other communities would subdivide into smaller groups of neighbours who would help each other during works construction.

There were clear advantages in maintaining early external control of project activities within organisationally weak and conflict-prone pastoral communities. However, communities must also feel they are both participating in the development decision-making and contributing in some way to the exercise of that control. Progressively, as they develop their capabilities, communities must also be able to take control themselves. In initially imposing its model of development, the project offered few choices to the co-operating communities. This observer, at least, felt some initial ambivalence regarding the rigid imposition of a 'community development' model on groups of people whose concepts of community differed so markedly from that of the model. However, for a culture undergoing stresses from forces of change such as settlement and severe soil erosion, new solutions are required. Ultimately the community-development model worked because, once they had the capabilities and the opportunity to do so, communities were able to manipulate and modify the model in a manner that suited their own needs.

The probable sustainability of project activities following the eventual departure of the Oxfam staff may be assessed at several levels. At the level of community organisational ability, after two years several communities were carrying out their soil and water conservation activities in the virtual absence of the project staff. Given adequate time and support from the project, the majority of communities would be capable of the on-going self-management of their erosion-control activities. At the technical and physical levels, after two years the project was still supplying the basic infrastructure necessary to carry out the erosion-control activities. This involved the provision of tools and the provision of a truck for transporting rocks. To increase the sustainability of community-implemented erosion-control works, the project encouraged local merchants to stock tools suitable for erosion control. It also started supplying some of the communities with donkey carts for rock transport. The premature forced closure of the project due to the outbreak of the Somali civil war meant that the effectiveness of these initiatives could not be assessed. Nevertheless after the start of the civil war and the rapid contraction of project activities, a number of communities continued their erosion-control works in the absence of the project's support and despite the obvious security risk to themselves. Thus some of the communities had developed a model of sustainable development that would enable them to continue to address their erosion problem after the departure of the project staff.

The question of impacts, both planned and unplanned, upon the development environment should be of concern to the evaluation of any project experience. This project's primary planned impact of developing communities' organisational capacity has been discussed. Of interest here is the nature of any unplanned impacts of the project's activities. The Oxfam intervention was technically simple and on a relatively small scale. Thus unplanned impacts were likely to be less in magnitude than those of a larger more complex intervention.

The major unplanned impact was the shift in community decision-making power away from the elders to the younger men in their dealings with the project. This unplanned impact was not discouraged by staff, because it was judged to contribute to the achievement of project goals.

A number of undesirable unplanned impacts were avoided because of the incremental nature of the planning process. Potential unplanned impacts and conflicts arose fairly often during the operation of the project. Undesirable unplanned impacts did not escalate, because of the locally intense and frequent monitoring of the outcomes of the project's initiatives. These monitoring procedures generally allowed the early identification and avoidance of unplanned impacts and conflicts before they could escalate into something unavoidable.

Conclusions

As regards the erosion-control component of the Erigavo Project, the Oxfam development style worked very effectively within a community-development environment. A development style which focused more on the form than on the process of development mighthave been less successful. For example, a more complex and larger intervention requiring sophisticated design technologies and bulldozer construction would have been largely irrelevant to the development environment. Its physical impact would probably have been shorter-lived, and the project would most likely have had little positive social development impact at all.

Oxfam's organisational concern was with the implementation of small-scale projects addressing simpler problems. This element of Oxfam's development style raises a broader issue that is relevant to the erosion-control component of the Erigavo Project.

As illustrated in Figure 4.2, the Erigavo Project was faced with a complex web of social, political, and physical interactions which was creating severe erosion problems. Clearly the project, with its simple community-based intervention, was doing little to confront the primary causes of the erosion problem which it was attempting to counteract. Looking at the erosion-control component of the project in isolation, one would have to question its relevance to the task of helping the pastoralists to adapt to the forces of change confronting them. Thus an over-simplistic definition of the problem may result in interventions which may appear to be sustainable in themselves. However, when examined in the light of broader processes and pressures on communities, such simple interventions may have limited sustainability, because they do not take into account these broader processes. In other words, while simple interventions may be more likely to achieve success, they may fail to address the complex problems confronting the communities at whom they are directed.

However, the poor record of more complex interventions should be recalled. In addition, the Erigavo erosion-control intervention achieved the development of community-based decision-making power structures which provided groups with the raw materials necessary to develop adaptive behavioural mechanisms. The challenge was to use these raw skills, developed through simple interventions which concentrated on the *processes* of development, to deal with more complex issues which also focused on the *form* of development being striven for.

This issue is examined further in relation to the rangeland-management component of the project.

6

Rangeland management and the Erigavo Project

Introduction

The Erigavo Project's rangeland-management component developed in response to broader social and political processes occurring in the Erigavo District. In recognising these processes, the shortcomings of the erosion-control component became clear. The soil and water conservation strategies were not only inadequate in the technical sense of failing to address the immediate physical causes of land degradation (i.e. overgrazing). They were also incapable of dealing with the primary non-physical causes of land degradation: their definition of causality and their subsequent approach to development were both very limited.

The project's rangeland-management component was thus initiated some time after the start of the erosion-control component. Once initiated, the two components were carried on concurrently and later acted as complements to one another.

The rangeland-management component may be divided into the following activities:

- establishing credibility and building community relationships;
- developing and presenting a programme of education, together with an associated information-exchange exercise;
- in conjunction with the communities, identifying appropriate rangeland-management strategies and impediments to the implementation of these strategies.

Building credibility and community relationships

There is one substantial difficulty associated with the implementation of any rangeland-management extension programme. This is that the costs of poor range management and the benefits of wise range management are difficult to predict with any accuracy, and take a considerable time to be expressed. For example, the reduction of livestock numbers or the reduction of grazing periods to encourage range regeneration in the Erigavo District may take years before any benefits become apparent, if at all. Thus rangeland extensionists are often faced with the task of attempting to convince pastoralists to adopt range-management strategies which have long benefit-return periods. The pastoralist is asked to discount the current costs of adopting the new strategy in deference to future ill-defined and unquantifiable benefits.

Pastoralists are pragmatists. They expect to experience immediate, tangible, and highly visible benefits from any programme with which they are involved. The project achieved the delivery of immediate and highly visible benefits through the implementation of three forms of community works. These were the construction of soil and water conservation structures; improvements to wells (with internal linings and external surrounding walls to prevent contamination by sediment, animal urine, and faeces); and the digging of berkets (reservoirs) for domestic water consumption. All these three developments were listed as high-priority needs by pastoral communities, and the berkets in particular were rated as a high priority by the pastoral women.

These three forms of community works were of considerable value to the rangeland-management component of the project. Each required a community to identify a common need, organise the labour and the timing of the construction, and develop and refine all the group decision-making processes required to do so. Improvements to wells in particular made a critical contribution to the development of group decision-making networks and group action. This later proved invaluable in providing communities with the ability to make broader decisions about the use of land. Unlike the erosion-control component which dealt with individual communities one at a time, the rangeland-management component had to encourage inter-community decision making about land use. Within the range-management arena, no community could operate in isolation. For a range-management strategy to be adopted, the majority of communities grazing an area would have to agree on it. To encourage general inter-community agreement on the critical land-use issues facing the pastoralists of the Erigavo District was an immensely complex and politically difficult task. It was also a task which could not be attempted without considerable preparatory work on relationship-building, both among the individual communities themselves, and between the communities and the project.

The exercise of well-improvement admirably suited the purpose of relationship-building. Well-improvements were considered a high-priority need by both male and female pastoralists. All communities who normally used a particular well were involved in both the decision making and the construction. The involvement required by all these communities helped to forge group decision-making frameworks which could later be employed for making communal decisions about the use of land. Nevertheless, the apparently simple task of well-improvements had to be approached cautiously and incrementally. Political relationships both between and within communities had to be taken into account. Both the costs and benefits of the well-improvements had to be seen to be evenly distributed by all those involved. The task of the project was to define and accommodate these political relationships. It had to ensure that all the costs (generally a portion of the construction costs) and benefits (equal access to the improved well) were seen to be evenly distributed. The value of well-improvements to the development of group decision-making frameworks was that they were highly visible: each time they watered their animals, the pastoralists were reminded of the benefits of achieving consensus; the benefits were relatively immediate (the construction usually taking only a few weeks, although the community preparation might take months); and ensuring equal access to the well clearly demonstrated to all the fair distribution of the benefits.

However, despite the potential benefits in terms of development, the political nature of access rights to water made well-improvements a highly risky form of development. Just how risky is best illustrated by the example of Hol Hol Well. On one occasion the project was approached by an important local government official requesting aid for the improvement of Hol Hol Well, 25 km from Erigavo. This official was ostensibly representing all the pastoralists who used the well. After the initial introduction from the official, project staff visited this well and spoke to elders believed to be the representatives of all the communities concerned. After a number of such meetings, agreement was reached on the provision of labour and the timing of the construction. One week before construction on the well site was to start, the project received a visit from a number of elders with whom it had not yet dealt. These elders claimed to represent other groups of well users (that is, other tribes) who had a long-running dispute with the group who had originally made contact with the project. These elders made it clear that the original group were planning to exploit the legitimacy provided by the involvement of the project, coupled with their well-improvement works, to lay claim to sole usage of the well. If this occurred, they argued, bloody conflict would erupt over ownership of the well. Discreet inquiries made by the Oxfam staff found all these claims to be true. It was also discovered that the local government representative who had made the original contact with the project was closely related to the group laying claim to the well. By his actions he was merely fulfilling his kinship obligations to his pastoral relatives. Needless to say, the project discreetly withdrew from this particular well-improvement scheme. Two weeks after this withdrawal, intense fighting over well-ownership erupted and ten pastoralists were severely wounded in knife and axe attacks. This example illustrates several important aspects of the social and political factors influencing pastoralists' decision making:

- that most Somalis, no matter what their educational or political achievements, will be strongly influenced in their decision making by their kinship obligations;

- that Somali pastoralists have a finely developed sense of political power-play, and frequently exploit this ability in their competition for resources;

- that the project itself, as a provider of resources, was regarded as having some degree of political power;

- that, in being perceived as having political power, the project was both vulnerable to exploitation and at the same time had the potential to wield this political power to achieve its objectives;

- that a knowledge of tribal relationships was crucial for any involvement by the project in decision making about erosion control, rangeland management, or land use.

The pastoralists' definition of the problem

The manner in which the problem was defined of course varied both between and within communities. It would also vary before and after contact with the project, and the presentation of the range-management education programme. It was a primary goal of this education programme to bring about a consensus between the communities and the project about the definition of the problems confronting the pastoralists. An additional project goal was to achieve general agreement between communities regarding the choice of solutions available to them. Ultimately it would be up to the communities to make these choices.

The pastoralists saw the process of settlement, and subsequent over-grazing, as the major cause of range degradation. The process of range privatisation (a distinction was generally made between the two processes) was viewed as having immense social (rather than environmental) costs. Notably, the process of pastoralist settlement, and the subsequent process of range privatisation, are not the same. Pastoralist settlement can and frequently does occur without the privatisation of the surrounding range areas. Range privatisation, not settlement itself, was the source of the grave social costs experienced by the Erigavo pastoralists. Both settlement and privatisation incurred environmental costs, however.

Pastoralists initially did not see vegetation loss as a precursor to the process of soil erosion. When asked what they thought the cause of the erosion was, their invariable and logical answer was 'the rain'. On-going contact with the project and the initiation of the education programme considerably changed the pastoralists' perceptions of the problem definition. They began to see the causal link between settlement, restrictions on traditional nomadic movements, vegetation loss, and soil erosion. When the discussion moved to the choice of land-management options which were available to them, they began to see the severe limitations that the privatisation of public grazing land placed upon the range of these choices. Ultimately the pastoralists defined the problem along three general lines:

- the social and environmental costs of the process of range privatisation (an issue of land tenure);
- the loss of valuable perennial pasture species, and the rapid rate of soil erosion, largely due to increased settlement (an issue of land management);

- the increasing susceptibility of the pastoralists and their animals to the effects of drought.

Potential solutions to the problem

The project began to seek agreement on the choice of potential solutions to the social and environmental problems confronting the Erigavo pastoralists.

This book has already identified the core problem at two levels: that of physical form, and that of social and political processes. The first level was associated with the immediate physical causes of the land-degradation processes affecting the Erigavo District. As described above, the project and the pastoralists ultimately reached agreement on this definition of this problem. The second level involved a recognition of the forces of change that were confronting the pastoralists of the District, and the pastoralists' inability to adapt quickly enough to these changes without incurring severe socio-cultural and environmental costs. Pastoralists (and indeed the project staff) began to appreciate this definition of the problem as they searched together for implementable solutions to the problems of range privatisation and land degradation. In searching for solutions, the pastoralists became acutely aware of the political powerlessness of their current position.

In early 1988 a meeting was held between the project, the elders representing the majority of those communities inhabiting the private rangelands, and a number of district and regional government officials. The intention of the meeting was to formalise an agreement on appropriate courses of action relating to land use and land tenure. Agreement was reached on the following courses of action.

- That each community inhabiting private range areas should relinquish private ownership and allow the range to return to its former public use. The support of the regional government administration should be sought in implementing and policing this reversion of land tenure.

- That the pastoralists who were denied their traditional access to grazing in the private range areas as they passed through during their nomadic herding movements would once again be allowed access.

- That the setting up of a rotational grazing reserve (or reserves) be investigated by the Oxfam project staff and community representatives. Grazing reserves, to be chosen on the basis of the likely regenerative capacity of the vegetation present, would also act as a reserve against drought. The communities would be responsible for the policing of the reserve and the choice of when to open it or close it to grazing.

However, for reasons described below, none of these actions was ever implemented.

The pastoralists chose to pursue the reversion of the range-privatisation process because of the heavy social and environmental costs of this change in land tenure. The reservation of public range from grazing, for either regenerative or drought-time grazing purposes, would be politically impossible while large areas of formerly public range were still held privately. Also pastoralists who did not hold private range areas would naturally resist any further locking up of public range while substantial areas of private range remained.

Nevertheless the elders recognised several critical impediments to the widespread adoption of this reversion process, and looked to the project to help them in overcoming these obstacles. These were:

- the difficulty of achieving consensus, both within and between communities, on appropriate courses of action;
- the transfer of decision-making power about land use from the communities to the government;
- an apparent lack of interest on behalf of the government in exercising this power.

Many pastoralists felt that if they relinquished their land unilaterally, would soon be seized by the non-participants. Secondly, in most communities there were more wealthy and politically powerful individuals who held very large tracts of private range. Some, but not all, of these individuals were vigorously resisting the reversion process. The transfer of decision-making power from communities to the government had made the task of overruling the politically powerful minority virtually impossible without strong and highly visible governmental support.

Considerable administrative and organisational steps were required to supervise and implement the reversion process. Many of these activities required widespread and simultaneous implementation. It was well beyond the ability of both the politically weak communities, and the small-scale Oxfam project, to undertake all the necessary steps. Clearly this was a role for government. The task of the project became that of encouraging government to undertake the role of managing the reversion.

The government was well aware of the social costs of the conflict over private range areas. Nevertheless, central and regional governments had historically given support to the range-privatisation process. They gave this support both directly and indirectly, through the initiation of ranch co-operatives, the selling of 'agricultural' titles for rangeland, and the offer of general policy support for pastoralist settlement.

The regional government was also aware of the significant community support for the reversion process. In response to an apparent ground-swell of community opinion, the government gave its overt endorsement. Privately, however, government officials remained unmoved by local representations, refusing to take any initiative in implementing the procedures requested of them, which involved giving political and legal support to the reversion process, declaring null and void all agricultural land-titles held over former public range, and refusing to accept claims over private range after a certain predetermined and widely publicised date.

Government inaction could be traced partly to pressure exerted by politically well-connected and powerful land-holders, and partly to the fact that the regional government primarily saw itself as a collector of taxes (most of which went to the capital, Mogadishu), rather than as a land-use policy maker or implementer. Essentially, regional government lacked the political and administrative means to make the changes in land tenure requested of it by the pastoral communities.

The project began investigating alternative courses of action, some involving government, some excluding government input. While the investigation of alternatives was in progress, the Somali civil war began and gradually the security situation within the Erigavo District deteriorated to such an extent that the project was compelled to close at the beginning of 1989. As is so often the case in Sahelian Africa, external political forces had substantial impacts on local development initiatives.

An evaluation of the project's rangeland-management activities

A number of project objectives were incrementally and progressively identified, and to a large extent they were achieved. They included defining the primary causes (both physical and non-physical) of land degradation evident within the Erigavo District; educating the pastoral communities to recognise these causes and their inter-relationships; and gaining a degree of agreement between the project and the communities on both the definitions of the problems and the choice of potential solutions. Very importantly, the project had developed replicable mechanisms for:

- contacting pastoralist communities;
- building up relationships of trust and effective communication mechanisms between itself and the communities;
- incrementally developing the organisational capacity and consensus-seeking behaviour of these communities.

When a number of pastoral communities had achieved a loose consensus on the definitions of the problem and the appropriate solutions to be adopted, it appeared that much of the project's development efforts had succeeded. The pastoral communities had achieved an excellent understanding of the causal processes and inter-relationships which had led to their current situation. An inter-community decision-making framework was effectively set up between a number of communities through the mechanisms of well-improvement schemes and the presentation of the range-management education programme. The fact that the elders representing the majority of pastoral communities could reach agreement on the politically sensitive issue of the reversion of the range-privatisation process was testimony to this achievement.

Ultimately what was lacking, however, was (on the part of the pastoralists) the power to make decisions about land use, and (on the part of the government) the political will to implement some of the chosen solutions. The government's inaction also highlighted the limited political power of the project at this level. While the project as a dispenser of resources held considerable political power at the level of individual local communities, it lacked influence over policy at the government level. This was because it was not seen as a dispenser of resources by government decision makers.

A strength of small-scale projects such as this is that their financial disbursements are small and they often act independently of government agencies. They are thus less prone to the deflection or interception of project resources by government elites. On the other hand, governments thus view small-scale projects as ineffectual political negotiators. Secondly, governments often define development in terms which differ from those of NGOs. The regional Somali government preferred capital-intensive infrastructural development. NGOs, on the other hand, are usually more concerned with social and political justice, which often entails a change in the balance of political power. Commonly this change in political power, either implicitly or explicitly, threatens government in some way. The regional government was certainly aware of the potential of the project's pastoral development initiatives to diminish its power base over time. The government was therefore unenthusiastic about supporting any initiatives which it could foresee would give greater power to pastoral communities.

Within the rangeland-management component, the project set in place much of the required framework for the development initiatives that were planned to follow. Yet the project did not achieve its broader and more fundamental objective: to aid the pastoral communities in adapting to the forces of change confronting them. This was to be achieved through providing them with the information and resources necessary to empower themselves to make behavioural choices which were technically, socially, and politically feasible.

The failure to secure this development goal can be explained from two perspectives. Firstly, the inherent impediments and complexities within the local pastoral environment made the planned socio-political development changes extremely difficult to achieve. This was undoubtedly true. Alternatively, the failure to achieve the desired development changes can be explained by the proposition that the Oxfam development style itself was ill-suited to addressing certain characteristics of this particular pastoral development environment.

The strengths and limitations of the Erigavo Project's development style

One particular characteristic that distinguishes pastoral environments from most other development environments is the nature of community interactions. Within the pastoral environment, communities (however one may define them) do not operate in isolation. The mobility of pastoralists and the fact that they, unlike sedentary agriculturalists, are in constant competition over livestock, pasture, water, or land, dictates that inter-community interactions must be a fundamental consideration within any development intervention. If planned change in some way impacts upon these interactions, then some form of consensus *between* communities must be achieved. There are many difficulties inherent in achieving this consensus. Firstly, a clear understanding of pastoralists' decision-making structures and influences is required, community-by-community, if interaction among them is a component of the planned change. Secondly, project staff must be prepared to act in any function that will help to achieve consensus between communities, whether it is in the role of teachers, manipulators, negotiators, advocates, or providers of physical resources. In practice, Erigavo Project staff found themselves fulfilling all of these development roles.

However, the complex pastoral planning environment highlights some of the shortcomings of a development style such as that employed in the original Erigavo Project. The small-scale community-development approach is specifically designed for interventions at the level of individual communities. For the same reason, project staff are normally limited in number, and project resources are deliberately limited to ensure the implementation of low-cost simple technologies.

The impacts of the project were thus limited by a number of characteristics, some inherent in Oxfam's development style, others components of the local development environment. The more important of these characteristics are listed below.

- The fact that several rival tribal groups traditionally competed both for grazing on the public range, as well as for ownership of private range, meant that reaching agreement between these groups was difficult.

- The increasing intrusion of the market economy into the area, coupled with range privatisation, meant that at least some of the extended family linkages had been weakened. Thus, for the elders, reaching agreement within their own communities was becoming a more difficult ask.

- The small scale of the Oxfam intervention limited the ability of the project to spread its contact and impacts on the broader geographical, social, and political fronts required. In particular the project could not deal simultaneously with all the pastoral communities required to reach agreement on questions of land use and land tenure. Thus while perhaps 30 community groups within the District had to reach some form of consensus on land use, the project found that it had the resources to deal only with four or five simultaneously with the intensity that was required to foster a constructive negotiation process.

Pastoral Development Planning

- The small scale of the Oxfam intervention also limited its abilities, both politically and functionally, to influence the government's land-use policy. The weakness of government structures meant that it could not accept responsibility for making decisions about land use (nor did it wish to). Nevertheless, government still retained enough power to preclude the pastoralists by force from regaining this responsibility. However, there were opportunities to modify government policy — although this would be a difficult task. The nature of the Oxfam intervention was such that it did not have the ability to influence government policy.

7

Identifying an appropriate model for pastoral development

Introduction

The historical record of pastoral development is poor. Much of this development was designed and implemented by governments. More recently, non-governmental organisations (NGOs) have become involved in pastoral development. Credit schemes, cereal banks, para-veterinary programmes, soil and water conservation projects, and post-drought restocking programmes have attracted particular attention. However, the Erigavo case study in the previous chapter cast doubt on the ability of one development approach to meet the broader development needs of pastoral communities.

Innovative development models are required to meet the requirements of pastoral peoples. Such models have yet to emerge from 40 years of government-sponsored development. If these models are to be found, they will probably emerge from the experimental development efforts of NGOs. However, NGOs must first critically examine the relevance of their current community-development models to the needs of pastoral peoples. They must also be willing to make the institutional behavioural changes necessary to adopt such models.

We have examined the characteristics of one pastoral development environment, and the strengths and limitations of Oxfam's development style in relation to the needs of that environment. Building on this learning experience, we will now briefly examine models of development which might be appropriate for meeting the needs of the pastoralists of the Erigavo District. In a number of ways the needs of the Erigavo pastoralists closely reflect the broader needs of many pastoral communities elsewhere. Thus in seeking development approaches which might meet the needs of the apparently intractable development problems encountered in the Erigavo District, we might identify certain principles which apply to other pastoral development environments.

The theoretical requirements of an appropriate development model

The theoretical comparative advantages of NGO interventions over those of government have been reported by Fowler (1990: 11), among others. Other writers[1] have questioned the degree to which these comparative advantages are actually achieved in practice. This unrealised potential should not be surprising to any who have worked within difficult and complex pastoral development environments.

The Erigavo Project fell short of its more optimistic objective of helping the pastoral communities to adapt to the forces of change confronting them, not least because of its premature closure in early 1989, enforced by the outbreak of the Somali civil war. However, many characteristics of the Erigavo Project development style were highly successful and worth preserving within any new model. These successes can be attributed to several key elements within the Project's development style: its flexibility and responsiveness, its incremental 'learning process' approach, its attention to the human or socio-political components of the development process, and its objective of developing the organisational capacity and co-operative behaviour of communities. Also, in a highly politically charged climate, the project was careful not to take any action that would allow it to be accused of tribalism, corruption, or bias in negotiations.

The characteristic that allowed the project to develop these key elements was the small scale of its intervention. Its limited size allowed the project the intensity of contact with the communities that was required. It ensured relative administrative and bureaucratic simplicity. It also ensured that whatever mistakes the project made were minor in scale. However, the small scale of the intervention also limited its ability to address both the magnitude of the problems confronting the pastoralists, and the magnitude of the development change required.

Thus the theoretical requirements of a development model relevant to the pastoral environment of the Erigavo District might include:

- a continuation, further testing, and extension of the successful features of the original Oxfam project, particularly the intensity and quality of the contacts between the project and the pastoral communities;
- a reconciliation of the apparent incompatibility between the need for *intensity* of contact with individual communities, and the need for community contacts and development changes on a significant *scale;*
- an increased political influence on the regional government's policies on decision making about the use of land;
- the need to ensure the sustainability of the development process.

Ultimately the responsibility for development change, if it is to be sustainable, must be taken on by indigenous institutions: indigenous government, indigenous NGOs, or local community organisations. Indigenous organisational structures within the Erigavo District presented few options. Regional government was financially, politically, and structurally very weak. No indigenous NGOs were operating within the region at this time. Local organisations were limited to the kinship ties of the extended family; or the loosely defined 'communities' encouraged by the project, based on an *ad hoc* mixture of kinship and geographical proximity. These local organisations would necessarily be an integral component of any sustainable development strategy. However, they were not immediately capable of accepting significant responsibility for development change without support from an external agency.

Government policy (or lack of policy) was intrinsically part of the development 'problem'. Thus there were clear political advantages in involving government as a joint stakeholder in planned development outcomes. However, this option was not immediately feasible. Dramatic improvements to the institutional strength and the absorptive capacity of the Somali government were required. This in turn depended upon a number of larger factors. Thus in the short-to-medium term, the operational development role for regional government within the Erigavo District would be limited.

Development models involving NGOs and local organisations

Given the weakness of indigenous government, the role of meeting the development needs of the Erigavo District pastoralists must fall to either NGOs or local organisations, or combinations of the two.

The Oxfam project had progressively identified a development approach that was responsive to the needs of the local pastoral environment. However, it lacked the elements of scale and macro-political influence required to achieve the desired development outcomes. Two models of development, the 'expanding NGO' model and the 'autonomous replicate' model, can be identified as potentially meeting the needs of the Erigavo pastoralists.

The 'expanding NGO' model

Faced with its limited scale and relative political powerlessness, there would have been apparent advantages in the Oxfam project scaling up to a much larger size. Firstly, it could have expected to contact and work with a much larger number of communities. Secondly, through the increase in financial disbursements and its more tangible presence within the District (or the Region), it could have expected to wield greater political bargaining power at the level of regional government.

However, the 'expanding NGO' approach would inevitably incur the kinds of costs that inevitably emerge from increasing the scale of an intervention: by employing more staff, increasing the number of activities, and spending more money, development agencies tend towards increasing complexity, bureaucracy, inflexibility, centralised decision making, unresponsiveness, and a diffusion of contact with proposed beneficiaries.

The 'expanded NGO' model might appear superficially to overcome many of the limitations of the original small-scale Oxfam intervention. It might also have found favour with both potential international donors and the Somali government. However, in implementing this model, many of the features which made the original intervention a success would be lost. There would be the danger of merely reproducing the conventional large-scale government-sponsored development intervention, with all of its much-chronicled problems and failings.

The 'autonomous replicate' model

It is suggested that an 'autonomous replicate' model of development (Figure 7.1) might fulfil the requirements (listed above) of an appropriate development model.

Identifying an appropriate model for pastoral development

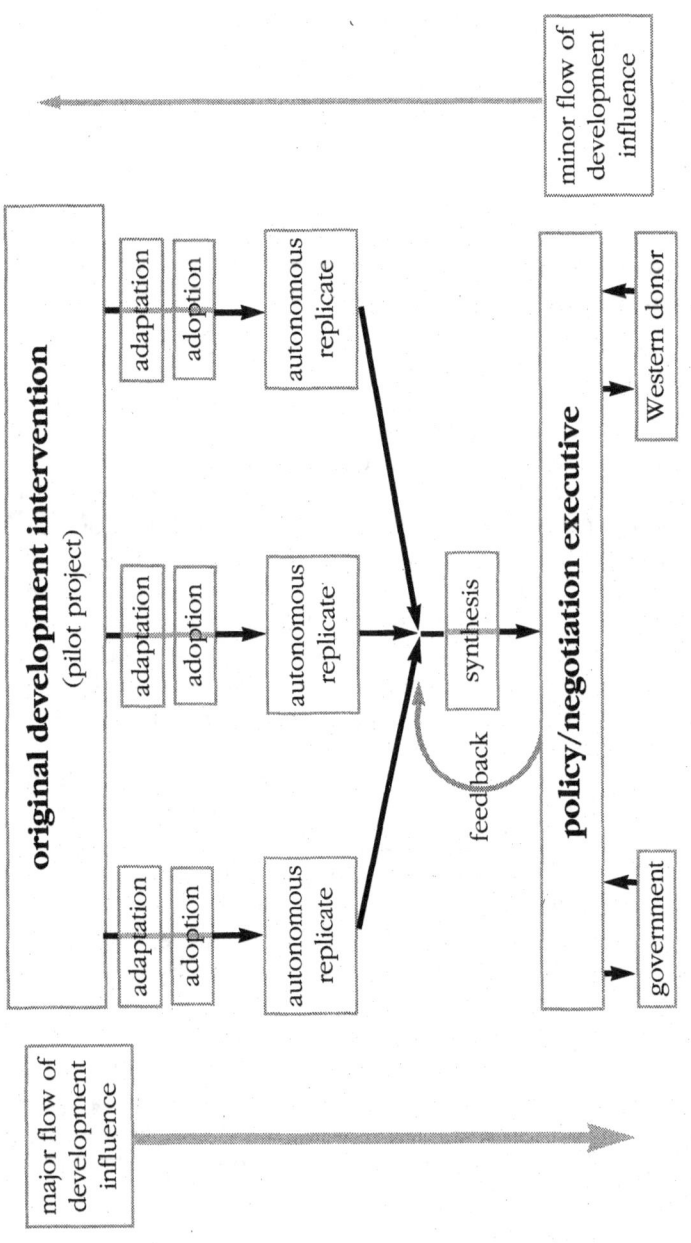

Figure 7.1: The 'autonomous replicate' model of development

A proposed initial organisational framework

An alternative to an NGO expanding the size of its original project would be to replicate the original. Rather than striving for one large project, the NGO would institute several small projects. These small projects might have been labelled 'para-replicates', because it is not intended that they exactly duplicate the efforts of the original pilot project. Rather, the small projects would try to emulate and improve upon the qualities of the original pilot project, and (ideally) retain those qualities which prove so elusive once increases in scale occur. They should not be attempting to duplicate the original exactly, because each development environment will have different requirements. Each of the replicates would be granted as much autonomy as the original project enjoyed. Centralised decision-making structures would be explicitly avoided, but some mechanism for co-operation and sharing of information and experiences would be adopted. Thus each project could maintain the intensity of relationship required between itself and its project partners, and respond accordingly to the unique conditions of the development environment within which it was working. The parent NGO could be satisfied that it was not compromising its ideological imperative, because each of the small projects would share a development policy framework. It could also feel that it was addressing a need or a problem on a scale that might have broader impacts outside the cluster of villages which were involved with the original project on which the replicates were modelled.

The appropriate organisational framework of the replicate approach is critical to the success of the model. A framework is sought which allows each replicate to operate with a considerable degree of autonomy. However, the framework must compel each replicate to provide feedback on the development learning-process, both to the other replicates and to a Policy Executive. The Policy Executive would be responsible for the two tasks of (firstly) translating the development needs of the replicates into policy, and (secondly) liaising and negotiating with government and influencing its policy direction. This model combines the flexibility of a networking process with the strategic focus provided by a more conventional corporate structure. However, the policy initiatives arise from the grassroots level of the replicates, rather than from the top — which is normally the case.

Thus the recurring conflict between scale and quality in development may potentially be resolved through the application of this model. Secondly, each autonomous unit can be viewed as a small replicated experiment in development. If all parties co-operate, the lessons learned, firstly from the original pilot project, and later by the autonomous units, will be shared among all the units. Thus the development learning-process may be rapidly speeded up. The framework therefore involves horizontal co-operation rather than a vertical administration. Sharing the development learning-process among replicates may also minimise the scale of the mistakes which are made.

So the 'autonomous replicate' model seeks to operate at both the local level of micro-development and the regional level of meso-development. Individually the replicates are involved in micro-development, in order to maintain the necessary intensity of contact between beneficiaries and project staff, and to optimise the development learning-process. However, through their networking framework, the replicates have the potential to be involved at the level of meso-development, in order to achieve the scale and complexity of development change that is required. Thus within this model, meso-development is firmly constructed on the experiences of micro-development and the needs of the pastoral communities. Here the Policy Executive (see Figure 7.1) plays a crucial role. It is responsible for facilitating the inter-replicate networking process and drawing out the meso-level development objectives which should be pursued.

All too often, large-scale pastoral development projects attempt macro-development, or meso-development, without the required micro-development taking place first. In such cases, the needs of pastoral communites remain unidentified, and the prerequisites of meso-development, such as strengthening the organisational capacity of pastoral communities, go unaddressed.

Each replicate should be viewed as an independent, separate, and self-directing development intervention. The replicates would not only facilitate development, negotiation, and consensus-seeking within the communities, and between the communities, with whom they interact. The replicates would also act as their advocates. This advocacy role would represent the pastoralists' interests not only before regional or national governments, but also perhaps before the donor agencies of international governments.

In many pastoral development environments, the relationship between the NGO and the indigenous government is crucial. Often the political and functional importance of this relationship is undervalued by both parties. In order to achieve a productive longer-term relationship with government, an NGO in principle has to achieve three objectives.

- It must demonstrate to the beneficiaries and government that it has the ability to achieve the development outcomes it promises. Most often these outcomes will involve improvements to the lot of poor, vulnerable, or disadvantaged groups. This process may also involve convincing government that the NGO as an agency of change has no implicit or explicit agendas that will ultimately be damaging to the government. This last case may be difficult to argue. By working for social and political justice, an NGO is by implication adversely influencing the power base of those elites who have good access to the government's decision-making systems. Indeed, the process of development change may be seen to be directly diminishing the power base of government itself.

- Secondly, the NGO must try to engage government as a joint stakeholder in the achievement of these planned outcomes.

- Thirdly, the NGO must enter into negotiations with government to improve the policy environment for facilitating the planned development changes.

Feedback and interaction between replicates is critical, not only to share lessons learned. Each of the communities/tribes which the replicates represent must reach consensus regarding land management, land tenure, and other associated issues. Achieving such consensus would be made easier by interaction among the replicates.

Given the history of tribal conflict in the Erigavo District, the difficulty of achieving intertribal consensus is considerable. However, the Oxfam project's success in involving rival tribes in well-improvement schemes demonstrated that normally adversarial tribes will, under particular circumstances, work together for a common goal. The preconditions for this collaboration are firstly that the costs and benefits (both short-term and long-term) must be seen to be evenly distributed among all tribes and all individuals. Secondly, the advantages in working inter-tribally rather than intra-tribally or individually must be clearly apparent. Such projects might save labour, for example; they might increase the participants' political power in the face of government; or it may merely be that the NGO decrees that, to attract its support and resources, some form of inter-tribal agreement or co-operation must occur. Inter-tribal and inter-community agreement

Identifying an appropriate model for pastoral development

regarding issues of land management and land tenure is critical. The technical aspects of the development process should be viewed as secondary concerns, as providing the means to the end of achieving this agreement. This is where the role of the replicates is concisely defined. The replicates must be seen by the various pastoral groups to be acting as third-party negotiators who understand and represent the needs of the pastoralists. The replicates' primary political imperative is the achievement of a workable consensus on crucial land-management and land-tenure issues. It is in the achievement of this understanding of the pastoralists' needs, and in the building of trust and communicative relationships between the pastoralists and the replicates, that the intensity of contact is most important.

The NGO replicates, taken as a whole, would attempt to act as a catalyst for a new social order which is necessary to confront and adapt to the forces of change affecting pastoralists such as those in the Erigavo District. On the other hand, as individual development projects, each of the replicates may act as an advocate for the interests of the handful of communities (or community sub-sets) whom it represents. Initially the individual replicates would accept this advocacy role in their capacity as internal organs within the NGO framework. Ultimately, however, the NGO (through its policy and negotiation executive) would act as an advocate for the composite or synthesised interests of all the communities represented. This process is illustrated in Figure 7.1.

The original Erigavo Project consisted of a project coordinator-technician, a male development officer, a female development officer, a part-time office administrator, and a driver mechanic. The project found that it could maintain the required intensity of contact with only four or five communities at any one time. There are approximately 30 functioning communities (the exact number would depend upon the definition of 'community' employed) within the private range areas. Thus around six autonomous project replicates would be required to support these communities in their policy-making about erosion control and land management. Thus the replicates would be asked:

- to seek community-development initiatives which would mitigate the land-degradation processes operating in the District;
- to try to address, therefore, the land-management and land-tenure issues which contribute to insupportable environmental and social costs;

- to adopt strategies which would build up the organisational strength and consensus-seeking behaviour of the communities, while at the same time identifying opportunities to encourage the communities to reach agreement on the key issues outlined above.

A crucial factor determining the success or failure of the 'autonomous replicate' model is the quality of the development staff employed within each replicate. Clearly the development employees must have the requisite technical skills, but — just as important — they must also have considerable negotiating skills, be extremely observant of *processes* in particular, be politically aware, be capable of working as part of a development team, and be capable of empathy with the needs of the target population. Finally, and very importantly, development workers must hold moral values and pursue development ideologies which are consistent with those of the agency with which they are working.

The 'autonomous replicate' model underlines the definition of development as a political process of strategic negotiation, a notion already highlighted by the original experience of the Erigavo Project! Conflict and negotiation would be expected at all levels: between sub-sets of the same community (men vs. women; young vs. old; poor vs. rich); between individual communities; between the communities and the NGO; between the NGO replicates as sub-projects competing for policy outcomes; and between all of the above and government.

The evolution and devolution of the organisational framework

An additional longer-term role for the international NGO would be organisation-building at two critical levels: that of the pastoral communities, and that of the local NGOs. Firstly, there is the need to support and develop the organisational capacity of the pastoral communities, in much the same way that the Erigavo Project demonstrated was possible. The organisational strength and consensus-seeking mechanisms developed by pastoral communities will largely determine the ultimate sustainability of planned development outcomes.

The NGO would be seeking to gradually devolve to the various pastoralist groups the activities originally carried out by the autonomous replicates. Each pastoral group would ultimately act as its own advocate and pressure group. However, the problem of maintaining agreement between traditionally adversarial tribes would probably remain a complex and difficult task for some considerable time. This role of negotiation and conciliation might have to continue to fall to an external body for some years. Given the structural weakness of government, the most appropriate body to accept this role would be an indigenous NGO which attempts to deal directly with the evolving local (probably tribally based) grassroots organisations.

The second level of organisation-building required of the development model would be to encourage indigenous NGOs. The genesis and development of local NGOs would allow them eventually to take over the operational role of the international NGO. At the time of this study, no indigenous NGOs were operating within the north of Somalia. In general, very few indigenous NGOs were in existence throughout the country. Those few which had developed were primarily based in Mogadishu under the watchful eye of the central government. The paucity of NGOs was largely a reflection of the government's negative policy on non-infrastructural development in general, and indigenous NGOs in particular.

The transfer of responsibility from international NGO to indigenous NGO is necessary for a long-term commitment from a development agency. It would be difficult to sustain long-term operational support of local community organisations by international NGOs. Thus the development of local NGOs would be actively encouraged by the international NGO. However, the local NGO must not be seen by either itself or the international NGO to be acting as merely a sub-contractor for its international counterpart, nor should it be viewed by donors as merely a conduit for the delivery of development funds to 'target' groups. Ultimately the local NGO must be in a position to be able to take on all the developmental and strategic organisational roles which were adopted by the original NGO. This is not to suggest that the local NGO must accept the *same* roles as the international NGO. Rather it must define its own roles.

However, given the negative attitude of the Somali government to development at the time of this study, the operational ability of a local NGO would have been severely restricted. Consequently within this model the international NGO must accept a nurturing role, to foster the developmental, organisational, and political strengths of embryonic indigenous NGOs until such time as this support is no longer necessary.

8

Conclusions: changing policy directions

New problem definitions and their policy implications for pastoral development

Clearly, much pastoral development has been largely irrelevant to the longer-term development needs of pastoral people. Historically, development policy has been aimed at 'improving' pastoralists' production mechanisms through technological change. The political component of development has almost entirely been ignored. It is only when technical interventions have had unforeseen political outcomes that *ex post* evaluations have identified the oversight. This somewhat patronising philosophy had assumed the beneficiaries to be trapped in a self-perpetuating, static environment of under-development. Yet the picture which has emerged from this discussion is quite different from this model. Rather than being passive victims of their environmental fate, pastoralists have developed over hundreds of years fine mechanisms of adaptation to highly variable climatic, social, and political environments. Pastoralists are familiar with having to adapt to rapid rates of change. The onset of drought signals not only climatic change but social and political change as well. Herds and families must often divide up and go separate ways. Political conflicts which escalate over rapidly diminishing reserves of pasture and water must be resolved one way or another. These adaptive mechanisms have been derived over generations of experience.

Conclusions: changing policy directions

As recently as the last few decades, many pastoral groups have been faced with immense modifications to their cultural environments. Pastoral cultures are having to confront recent and rapid forces of change such as land degradation, increasing population densities, lowered mobility, the intrusion of market economies, increasing pressures on kinship relationships, increasing vulnerability to drought, and the displacement of poorer pastoralists from the pastoral economy. The problems besetting pastoral groups as a result are not due to ignorance or mismanagement, but to an inability to adapt rapidly enough to these modifications to their social, political, and physical environments. For example, recent sociopolitical changes have wrought disastrous consequences in causing the breakdown of traditional drought-coping mechanisms among the Turkana of northern Kenya (McCabe 1990).

For many pastoral environments the focus of development policy requires redefinition. No longer should development policy be viewed as being concerned merely with the transfer of technology. Development policy should be revalued to recognise that it is not merely improved technology that pastoralists require or desire. More importantly, pastoralists need help in developing cultural mechanisms -- technical, social, and political -- which will allow them to adapt to rates of change, or types of change, with which they have never previously had to cope.

In the pastoral context, development should be viewed not as technological change but as *adaptive change*. In some instances the necessary development intervention will be technical, but rarely will this be the sole requirement. More frequently, social and political interventions will be required, in association with others of a technical nature. The appropriate forms of adaptive development will be specific to the individual situation, as each pastoral environment will be different. Yet despite this apparent need, there has been an almost complete absence of development policies, programmes, and projects specifically designed to help pastoral communities to cope with, and adapt to, these pressures.

New directions for pastoral development policy

The foregoing discussion and the recently emerging literature suggest a number of high-priority policies.

Reducing the vulnerability of pastoral communities

The most urgent need is to reduce the vulnerability of pastoral communities. Programmes directed at alleviating pastoralists' vulnerability to poverty, drought, and famine are almost completely absent from the development record. Sadly there appears to be a continuing tendency in government agencies to view drought and famine as 'disasters' which can be neither prevented nor mitigated, rather than as recurring events to which alternatives might be developed. An apparent inability of development policy to come to grips with the vulnerability of pastoral communities means that there continues to be a passive acceptance of the 'inevitability' of famine. The corollary to this perceived inevitability is a continuing reliance upon emergency-relief food aid as the solution to famine, accompanied by widespread suffering once the disasters have begun. Clearly, famine-relevant policy is urgently required in the areas of agriculture, livestock, and infrastructural development.

A number of predisposing factors have been identified as being critical to the occurrence of famine (Curtis *et al* 1988). The most important are a lack of food security, poor infrastructure and communications, low import-capacity and high debt-burdens, political instability, and a large vulnerable population. It is worth emphasising that food insecurity has socio-political as well as bio-physical causes. With these precursors in place, famine is simply waiting to happen, with drought and war (particularly when they occur in concert) acting as mere triggers (see Figure 8.1). However, all these factors can potentially be addressed through appropriate development policies.

We can identify a number of areas deserving urgent attention which might potentially contribute to reducing pastoral communities' vulnerability to famine:

- Development of response-related infrastructure and communications.
- Development of responsible and responsive government bureaucracies.
- Improvements to food production (food crops rather than cash crops; soil and water conservation interventions).
- Strengthening of traditional livestock-production systems.
- Development of appropriate and culturally acceptable credit schemes.
- Decentralised community-based food-security systems.
- Decentralised Famine Early Warning Systems (FEWS).

Conclusions: changing policy directions

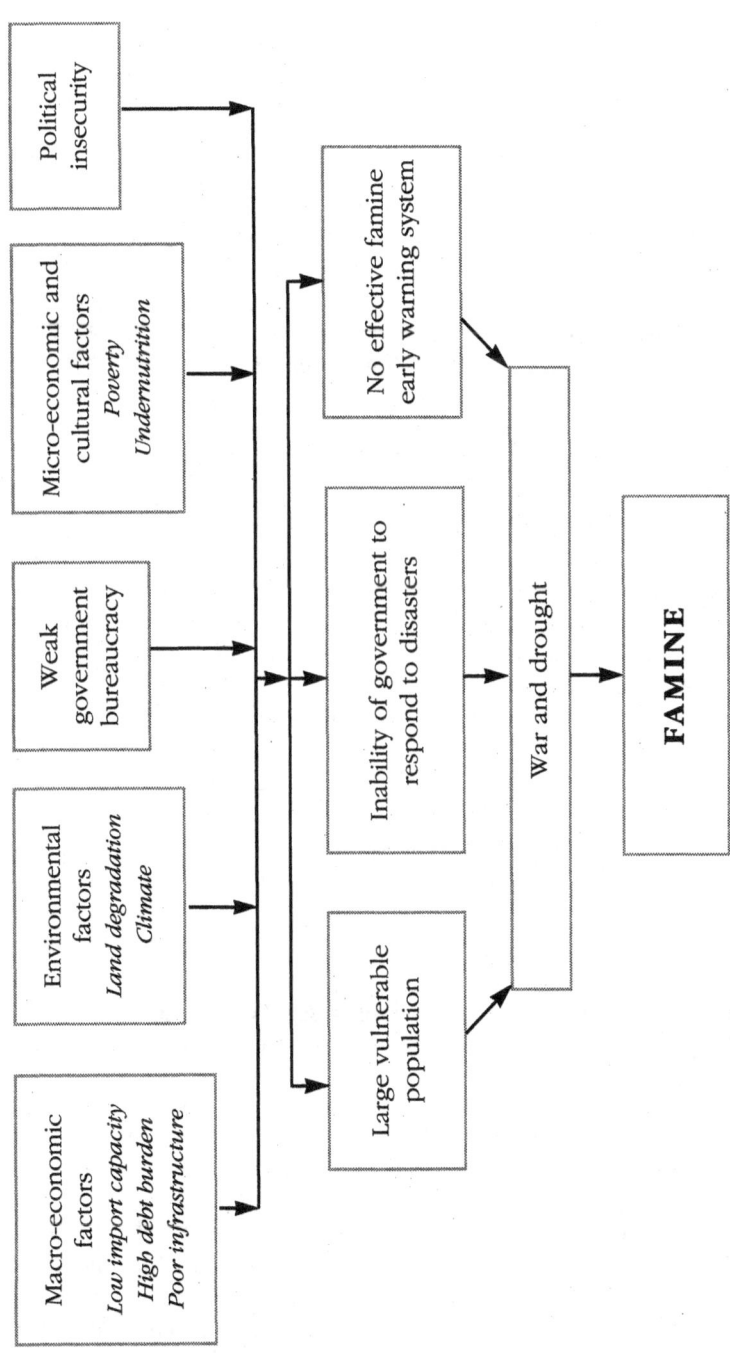

Figure 8.1: *Predisposing factors and triggers of famine in vulnerable populations: war and drought are not the primary causes of famine, but only the secondary triggers.*

Pastoral Development Planning

- Improvements to food-storage capabilities (e.g. grain banks).
- Development support for moves towards democratic government.
- Development support for a free press.
- Limitations on military aid to dictatorial regimes.
- Relief from debt burdens.

Clearly the final four initiatives are highly politicised and may be extremely difficult to achieve. Nevertheless it can be argued that often the development policy of aid agencies has supported the political and macro-economic *status quo* in a number of countries. In doing so, development policy has implicitly worked towards increasing the vulnerability of pastoral communities. It is time that this trend was reversed: development policy must work towards political change that contributes to the survival of pastoral communities rather than their demise. If development can support political change in one direction where pastoral peoples are increasingly disadvantaged, it can also work towards political change in the other direction in order to improve their lot.

Vulnerability is such a fundamental issue in pastoral development and the future of pastoral peoples that there is a compelling argument that all pastoral development interventions should be valued in terms of their contribution to reducing communities' vulnerability. The short sharp message here is that increases in productivity, so often the primary objective of technologically focused development, do not on their own guarantee reductions in communities' vulnerability. Increases in production decrease vulnerability only when those increases are available to poor groups, and when the benefits of extra production can be stored in some persistent and easily accessible form.

Increasing the security of pastoralists' land tenure and mobility, and ensuring access to pasture and water

Earlier we considered the loss of traditional pastoral land to other competing uses such as agriculture, ranching, urban development, conservation, and tourism. We also noted the contribution of this loss to increasing pastoral population densities, land degradation, and pastoral communities' susceptibility to poverty and famine. Development has historically encouraged the transfer of land from pastoral use to more financially rewarding uses, and more politically powerful land users. What is now required is the protection of better-

Conclusions: changing policy directions

quality pastoral land from annexation for non-pastoral uses, unless the indigenous pastoral people support, and are participants in, a change in land use.

Another area deserving attention is the need to re-establish the seasonal mobility of pastoralists across regional and national boundaries — rather than support for the settlement and sedentarisation of pastoralists typified by interventions such as ranching schemes.

Increasing attention is being directed, somewhat belatedly, to the question of pastoral land-tenure and mobility, with many observers[1] calling for the protection of pastoralists' land-use rights. Others have drawn attention to the links between political insecurity and land degradation.[2] This attention, though promising, is yet to be translated into government development policy.

Alternative employment programmes

Given recent history, we can expect the recurring marginalisation of poorer pastoralists and the displacement of increasing numbers of these pastoralists from pastoral production. What is required is investigation of, and governmental support for, non-pastoral employment opportunities for pastoral groups who are forced to leave their traditional sector. The result of inaction is clearly evident in the slums of a number of African cities, as displaced pastoralists move to join the increasing pool of urban poor. Post-drought restocking schemes maintain the near-viable commodities in pastoral production and help to reduce the numbers of those displaced. However, restocking schemes are generally inappropriate for large groups of severely marginalised pastoralists, owing to the magnitude of investment required to return such groups to viable levels of production.

Improved education and health services

Education and health services in remote pastoral areas are notoriously poor. The urban bias in development is clearly evident in the provision of education and health. Poor education and health services in pastoral areas are of concern not only because of the failure to provide for basic human needs: they also contribute to the political powerlessness of pastoral peoples. Pastoral communities which are poorly educated or debilitated by inadequate medical care or nutrition are less able to compete, or argue their case, within the political decision-making processes which influence their future livelihoods.

Improvements to security

Poor security debilitates pastoral communities in a number of ways. Lessened mobility, livestock thefts, loss of human life, inability to engage in opportunistic agriculture, increased over-grazing and land degradation, and increased vulnerability to drought and famine are all potential impacts of poor security. Development policy-makers have yet to identify security in pastoral areas as a development issue. In fact it can be argued that in some countries development has historically contributed to increased insecurity. In such cases the provision of extensive military aid has allowed the establishment and maintenance of authoritarian states whose concern is the domination of pastoral groups, rather than their protection.

Pastoralist settlement as a development issue

While many development exercises designed to force, coerce, or entice pastoralists to settle have either failed or had adverse unplanned outcomes, an increasing number of pastoral communities have spontaneously settled of their own accord. From the policy perspective there is a need to view the process of pastoralist settlement as a development *issue* rather than merely as a development *outcome*. Further research is required into the reasons why pastoral groups settle, and the impacts that settlement has upon such characteristics as traditional cultural adaptive mechanisms, kinship ties, subsistence and market values, and demographic parameters — among others.

Development policy must recognise and address the primary causes of land degradation

At the project level, there must be a recognition and treatment of the *primary* (often social and political) causes of pastoralist poverty and land degradation — as opposed to the commonly attempted treatment of the secondary causes and symptoms of land degradation. Projects which attempt to address land degradation through grazing management, livestock reduction, or ranching schemes, when the causes are increased human-subsistence requirements and/or decreased availability of grazing areas, are ultimately doomed to failure. Community training for soil and water conservation using low-cost, appropriate technologies which can be implemented and maintained by the beneficiaries themselves have demonstrated some successes. While not addressing primary causes, such activities can buy time for pastoral communities in mitigating land-degradation processes.

Adaptive social and political strategies rather than technological 'solutions'

At the community level, strong, on-going, external support is required to enable pastoral groups to undertake individual adaptive action. The support required will rarely be technical alone. More frequently it will entail social, economic, and political guidance for pastoral groups, attempting firstly to identify, and eventually to choose from, alternative courses of action. External support may be provided by government, NGOs, or appropriate local rural organisations. Eventually such supporters may be called upon to play the role of external advocates for pastoral communities.

When contemplating pastoral development, no longer should the primary concern be the implementation of the Western 'productivity improvement' model in the pastoral sector. Nor should the design of development interventions continue to be driven by whatever Western technology or model of livestock development happens to be in vogue. Rather, development agencies must re-examine the manner in which they define the development needs of pastoral people. Development agencies must respect the pastoralists' need for independence, and their traditional resilience in the face of recurring adversity and the rapidly encroaching forces of change. Their cultural needs must be satisfied with appropriate and sustainable development methodologies.

Ultimately it will be the poorer pastoralists, with their ever-diminishing access to public range and the better pastures, who are least equipped to respond positively to these recent changes in the pastoral political economy. Pastoral development policy should be aimed at providing disadvantaged pastoral groups with the skills and resources required so that *they* can make the behavioural choices necessary to adapt and survive within their new environments.

Advocacy roles for NGOs

In the West it has long been accepted that disadvantaged groups need advocates willing to argue their case before the political decision-making bodies. Those taking on the advocacy role must be politically aware, articulate, resourceful, and able to represent accurately the needs and wishes of the disadvantaged groups whom they represent. Within pastoral development, NGOs in particular are well placed to take on this advocacy role.[3] As NGOs become increasingly involved in pastoral development, they form intimate relationships with their pastoral clients, and are intensely concerned with the identification and articulation of community needs. These new advocacy roles will require an adjustment in the focus of NGOs. While NGO-style micro-development is essentially inward-looking in terms of building up the capacities of local communities, advocacy roles require an outward focus, whereby the external pressures and concerns are confronted. This role is politically sensitive in the extreme, as NGOs' and churches' experience of advocacy in South and Central America has illustrated. To act as effective advocates, NGOs must be prepared to form inter-agency networks whereby individual, isolated efforts can be brought together to form a more cohesive and politically effective force. However, NGOs have a poor record of interagency co-operation and co-ordination. While there may be good reasons for NGOs maintaining their independence from one another in pursuing their individual models of development, co-operation is essential in order to influence political decision-making processes in favour of their pastoral clients. Nevertheless if NGOs do not take up this politically difficult and potentially dangerous task of advocacy, who else will argue the pastoralists' case before indifferent national governments and international development agencies?

Conclusions

This book has canvassed some of the issues which deserve to be part of the debate about pastoral development policy. But in many ways this debate has yet to happen in any serious fashion. Historically, pastoral development policy has been too narrowly focused. Often policy has primarily reflected the needs of development agencies or governments, rather than the needs of pastoral communities themselves. Yet the identification of appropriate development policy is crucial for the future of pastoral communities. Policies are the points on the horizon upon which we take our compass bearings, and they give us the the

Conclusions: changing policy directions

means to measure our progress. All pastoral development workers are acutely aware of the difficulties of the political, technical, and cultural topography which must be traversed. Often in development we become so preoccupied with the difficulties of the terrain that we neglect to critically appraise the direction in which we are heading.

For many pastoral environments, the focus of development policy requires redefinition. No longer should policy be viewed as being concerned merely with technology transfer. Development policy should be revalued to incorporate the recognition that it is not merely improved technology that pastoralists require or desire. More importantly, pastoralists need help to develop cultural mechanisms — technical, social and political — which will allow them to adapt to rates of change, or types of change, with which they have never previously had to cope.

Pastoral development should thus be viewed not as technological change but as *adaptive change*. In some instances the necessary development intervention will be technical, but this will rarely be the sole requirement. More frequently, social and political interventions will be required, in association with those of a technical nature. The appropriate forms of adaptive development will be situation-specific, because each pastoral environment will be different.

Adaptive development requires the co-operation of both government and NGOs, each seeking to make a contribution in areas in which they can claim comparative advantage. Because they have such an important contribution to make, NGOs in particular face enormous challenges when they move into pastoral development. They have crucial roles to play as development experimenters, as negotiators, as community advocates, and as identifiers of the needs of the poor and vulnerable. In meeting these challenges, NGOs will aslo need to accept behavioural changes required by their exploration of new models of pastoral development. At the same time, they must retain those characteristics of human-scale development, of flexibility and responsiveness, which have proven so successful in other development environments. For their part, governments must be prepared to give support to and learn from the NGO experience, without detracting from NGOs' autonomy -- although this balance will often be difficult to achieve.

Sadly, if past trends continue, the future for pastoral peoples is grim. Nowhere has current development practice proved so inadequate as it has with the pastoral development environment. Nowhere is the need for innovative approaches to development more pressing, and nowhere is the time available to discover these new directions so limited.

Notes

Chapter 2

1 Sandford 1976; Swift 1977, 1982.
2 Swift 1982.
3 Kitching 1983; Meir 1986; Hill 1988; Iliffe 1989.
4 Hemming 1966:192 3.
5 For example, Simpson 1984.
6 Sandford 1976; Salih 1978; Swift 1982.
7 Swift 1976, 1977, 1982; Salzman 1980; Reusse 1982; Hogg 1986; Behnke 1986, 1987, 1988.
8 Behnke 1986, 1988; Swift 1976; Reusse 1982.
9 Hogg 1986.
10 Sutter 1987.
11 Sikana and Kerven 1991.
12 For example, USAID 1972, 1973; Rapp 1976; le Houérou 1977; UN 1977a, 1977b; Baker 1980.
13 For example, Sandford 1983:12-16.
14 For example, see Heady 1975.
15 For an empirical study within African ecosystems which supports this thesis, see Bosch 1989.
16 For example, see Behnke and Scoones 1992.
17 See Blaikie 1989:23-4.

Chapter 3

1 Goldschmidt 1981:104-5; Gall 1982:30; Valentin 1985.
2 Sandford 1983:81.
3 Rogers and Randolph 1988: 58.

Notes

4 Gall 1982: 22.
5 ILCA 1979; Trail and Gregory 1984: 109; Carew *et al.* 1986: 2.
6 Hogg 1987.
7 Dahl and Hjort 1976: 24; White and Meadows 1981; de Ridder and Wagenaar 1986.
8 Goldschmidt 1981: 114-15; Gall 1982: 48; Bekure and McDonald 1985.
9 Driscoll 1967; Wilson 1977; Wilson *et al.* 1984; Sweet 1986.
10 Williams 1974; Hyder and Bement 1977; Harrington 1981.
11 Blaikie 1985, 1989; Blaikie and Brookfield 1987; Prior 1992a.
12 McCarthy *et al.* 1985; IFAD 1986; Pacey and Cullis 1986; Park 1986; Reij 1987, 1988.
13 IFAD 1986: 13-28; Prior 1992b.
14 Goldschmidt 1981; Sandford 1983.
15 Baldus 1977; Galaty 1980; Goldschmidt 1981: 109-14; Oxby 1985.
16 Herskovits 1926; Dyson-Hudson and Dyson-Hudson 1969.
17 Schneider 1984.
18 UN Economic Commission for Africa 1985: 12-13.
19 Pratt and Gwynne 1977: 76.
20 Simpson 1984.
21 Stiles 1981: 373; Prior 1992a.
22 Hama 1981: 244-50; Prior 1992a.
23 Schneider 1981.
24 Breman *et al.* 1978; Draz 1978; Odell 1982; Batanouny 1986; Shepherd 1988.
25 Hopcraft 1981; Sandford 1983: 118-22.
26 Sandford 1983: 3-4; Behnke and Scoones 1992.
27 Sandford 1983: 124-6; Behnke 1987.
28 Hudson 1987; although see also Hudson 1992 for a dramatic shift in emphasis towards social concerns.
29 IFAD 1986: 58-66.
30 McCarthy *et al.* 1985.
31 Younger and Bonkoungou 1989; Critchley 1991.
32 Dieye 1989; Gonda 1989; Almond 1987; Sandford 1981; Sollod *et al.* 1984.
33 Almond 1987; Gonda 1989.
34 Moremi 1990.
35 Fulton and Winter 1988: 10-11.
36 White 1984; Hogg 1985; Toulmin 1986; Moris 1988.
37 Oakley and Marsden 1984; Oakley 1991.
38 Chambers and Ghildyal 1985; Chambers *et al.* 1989; Critchley 1991.

39 McCarthy *et al.* 1985: 11; IFAD 1986; Reij 1988.
40 Personal communication from CRDP staff.
41 Zeissan 1986.
42 Weiner 1984.
43 Cassen 1986: 128.
44 Lappé *et al.* 1981.
45 For example, World Bank 1989b.

Chapter 5

1 See also Rondinelli 1983 and Uphoff 1990 for similar approaches.

Chapter 7

1 Tendler 1982; Allen 1990; Brown 1990.

Chapter 8

1 Oxby 1989; Lane and Swift 1989; Baxter and Hogg 1990, IIED 1991; Cullis 1992.
2 Hjort af Ornas 1990.
3 Prior 1992a; Cullis 1992.

References

Allen, T. (1990), 'Putting people first again: non-governmental organisations and the "new orthodoxy" in development', *Disasters* 14/1: 63-8.

Almond, M. (1987), *A Para-Vet Programme in South Sudan*, Overseas Development Institute Pastoral Development Network Paper 24c, London: ODI.

Arnstein, S.R. (1969), 'A ladder of citizen participation', *American Institute of Planners Journal* 31: 331-8.

Baker, R. (1975), 'Development and the pastoral peoples of Karamoja, Northeastern Uganda: an example of the treatment of symptoms', in T. Monod (ed.): *Pastoralism in Tropical Africa*, pp.187-205, London: Oxford University Press.

Baker, R. (1980), *Desertification: Cause and Control. A Study of the UN Plan of Action and its Possible Application*, Development Studies Occasional Paper No. 6, Norwich: University of East Anglia.

Baldus, R.D. (1977), 'The introduction of co-operative livestock husbandry in Tanzania', in *FAO Land Reform*, Rome: FAO.

Batanouny, K.H. (1986), 'Rangelands of Arabian Peninsula with a special reference to the history of range management (the Hema, an old Arabian reserve system)', in P.J. Joss, P.W. Lynch, and O.B. Williams (eds): *Proceedings of the Second International Rangeland Congress*, pp. 234-5, Canberra: Australian Academy of Science.

Baxter, P.T.W. and **R. Hogg** (1990), *Poverty, Property and People: Changing Rights in Property and Problems of Pastoral Development*, Manchester: Department of Social Anthropology and International Development Centre, University of Manchester.

Behnke, Roy (1986), *The Implications of Spontaneous Range Enclosure for African Livestock Development Policy*, ALPAN Network Paper 12, Addis Ababa: International Livestock Centre for Africa.

Behnke, Roy (1987), 'Cattle accumulation and the commercialisation of the traditional livestock in Botswana', *Agricultural Systems* 24: 1-29.

Behnke, Roy (1988), *Range Enclosure in Central Somalia*, Overseas Development Institute Pastoral Development Network Paper 25b, London: ODI.

Behnke, Roy, and I. Scoones (1992), *Rethinking Range Ecology: Implications for Range Management in Africa*. Environment Working Paper No. 53, Washington: World Bank.

Bekure, S. and I. McDonald (1985), *Some Policy Issues of Livestock Marketing in Africa*, ALPAN Network Paper 2, Addis Ababa: International Livestock Centre for Africa.

Blaikie, P. (1985), *The Political Economy of Soil Erosion in Developing Countries*, London: Longman.

Blaikie, P. (1989), 'Explanation and policy in land degradation and rehabilitation for developing countries', *Land Degradation and Rehabilitation* 1: 23-37.

Blaikie, P. and H. Brookfield (1987), *Land Degradation and Society*, London: Methuen.

Bosch, O.J.H. (1989), 'Degradation of the semi-arid grasslands of southern Africa', *Journal of Arid Environments* 16: 165-75.

Breman, H., A. Diallo, G. Traore, and M.M. Djiteye (1978), 'The ecology of the Annual Migrations of Cattle in the Sahel', in *Proceedings of the First International Rangeland Congress*, Denver, Denver: Society for Range Management, pp. 592-5.

Brown, D. (1990), 'Rhetoric or reality? Assessing the role of NGOs as agencies of grassroots development', *University of Reading Agricultural Extension and Rural Development Unit Bulletin* 15: 3-10.

Burke, K. (1990), 'Property rights in "animals of strangers": notes on a restocking programme in Turkana, NW Kenya', in Baxter and Hogg 1990, pp.129-36.

Carew, S.F., J. Sandford, Y.J. Wissocq, J. Durkin, and J.C.M. Trail (1986), 'N'Dama cattle productivity at Teko Livestock Station, Sierra Leone and initial results from crossbreeding with Sahiwal', *ILCA Bulletin* 23: 2-10.

Casley, D.J. and K. Kumar (1988), *The Collection, Analysis and Use of Monitoring and Evaluation Data*, Baltimore: John Hopkins University Press.

Cassen, R. (1986), *Does Aid Work?* (second edition, 1993), Oxford: Clarendon Press.

Chambers, R. (1983), *Rural Development: Putting the Last First*, Harlow, Essex: Longman Scientific.

Chambers, R. (1985), *Managing Rural Development: Ideas and Experience from East Africa*, West Hartford: Kumarian Press.

Chambers, R. and B.P. Ghildyal (1985), 'Agricultural research for resource-

References

poor farmers: the farmer-first-and-last model', *Agricultural Administration and Extension* 20: 1-30.

Chambers, R., A. Pacey, and **L.A. Thrupp** (1989), *Farmer First: Farmer Innovation and Agricultural Research*, London: Intermediate Technology.

Commonwealth of Australia (1984), *Report of the Committee to Review the Australian Overseas Aid Program*, Canberra: Australian Government Publishing Service.

Critchley, W. (1991), *Looking After Our Land: New Approaches to Soil and Water Conservation in Dryland Africa*, Oxford: Oxfam (UK and Ireland).

Cullis, A. (1992), *Taking the Bull by the Horns: NGOs and Pastoralists in Coalition*, Overseas Development Institute Pastoral Development Network Paper 33d, London: ODI.

Curtis, D., M. Hubbard and **A. Shepherd** (1988), *Preventing Famine: Policies and Prospects for Africa*, London: Routledge.

Dahl, G. (1979), *Suffering Grass: Subsistence and Society of Waso Borana*, Stockholm: Department of Social Anthropology, University of Stockholm.

Dahl, G. and **A. Hjort** (1976), *Having Herds: Pastoral Herd Growth and Household Economy*, Stockholm: Department of Anthropology, University of Stockholm.

Dieye, N. (1989), 'The paravet project of Loumboul Samba Abdoul, Senegal', *Baobab* 2: 19.

Doran, M.H., A.R.C. Low, and **A.L. Kemp**, (1979), 'Cattle as a store of wealth in Swaziland: implications for livestock development and overgrazing in Eastern and Southern Africa', *American Journal of Agricultural Economics* 16: 37-41.

Draz, O. (1978), 'Revival of the Hema system of range reserves as a basis for the Syrian Range Development Program', *Proceedings of the First International Rangeland Congress*, Denver, Denver: Society for Range Management, pp. 100-103.

Driscoll, R.S. (1967), 'Managing public rangelands: effective livestock grazing practices and systems for national forests and national grasslands', US Department of Agriculture, AIB-315 (original not seen).

Dyson-Hudson, R. and **N. Dyson-Hudson** (1969), 'Subsistence herding in Uganda', *Scientific American* 220/2: 76-80.

Evangelou, P. (1984), 'Cattle marketing efficiency in Kenya's Maasailand', in Simpson and Evangelou 1984, pp. 123-41.

Fowler, A. (1990), 'Doing it better? Where and how NGOs have a "comparative advantage" in facilitating development', *University of Reading Agricultural Extension and Rural Development Unit Bulletin* 15: 11-20.

Fry, P. (1988), 'Evaluation of Oxfam's Four Restocking Projects in Kenya', Oxford: Oxfam.

Fulton, D. and **M. Winter** (1988), 'Why don't cereal banks work as they are supposed to?', *Baobab* 1: 8-11.

Galaty, J.G. (1980), 'The Maasai group ranch: politics and development in an African pastoral society', in P.C. Salzman (ed.): *When Nomads Settle: Processes of Sedentarisation as Adaptation and Response*, pp.157-72, New York: Praeger.

Galaty, J.G., D. Aronson, and **P.C. Salzman** (eds.) (1981), *The Future of Pastoral Peoples*, proceedings of a conference held in Nairobi, 4-8 August 1980, Ottawa: International Development Research Centre.

Gall, P. (1982), *Strategies for Dealing with Rangeland Management Problems*, Washington: Chemonics International Consulting Division and USAID.

Goldschmidt, W. (1981), 'The failure of economic pastoral development programs in Africa', in Galaty, Aronson and Salzman (eds.) 1980, pp. 101-18.

Gonda, S. (1989), 'Paravet work in South Sudan', *Baobab* 2: 16-18.

Gwyer, G.D., and **J.C.H. Morris** (1983), 'Natural resources', in B.E. Cracknell (ed.): *The Evaluation of Aid Projects and Programmes*, Proceedings of a Conference organised by ODA and the Institute of Development Studies at the University of Sussex 7-8 April 1983, pp. 44-63, London: Overseas Development Administration.

Hama, A. (1981), 'Consumption and marketing of pastoral products among the Kal Tamacheq in the Niger Bend, Mali', in Galaty *et al.* (eds.) 1981, pp. 244-50.

Hardin, G. (1968), 'The tragedy of the commons', *Science* 162: 1243-8.

Harrington, G.N. (1981), 'Concepts and methods in the study of natural grazing land management', in E.K. Christie (ed.): *Desertification of Arid and Semiarid Natural Grazing Lands*, Vol. I: Review Papers, Australian Development Assistance Bureau and School of Australian Environmental Studies, Griffith University.

Harrington, G.N., M.H. Friedel, K.C. Hodgkinson, and **J.C. Noble** (1984): 'Vegetation ecology and management', in G.N. Harrington, A.D. Wilson and M.D. Young (eds.): *Management of Australia's Rangelands* pp. 41-61, Canberra: CSIRO.

Heady, H.F. (1975), *Rangeland Management*, New York: McGraw-Hill.

Hemming, C.F. (1966), 'The vegetation of the northern region of the Somali Republic', *Proc. Linn. Soc. Lond.* 177/2: 173-249.

Herskovits, M.J. (1926), 'The cattle complex in East Africa', *American Anthropologist* 28: 230-72, 361-88, 494-528, 633-44.

Hesse, C. (1987), *Livestock Market Data as an Early Warning Indicator of Stress in the Pastoral Economy*, Overseas Development Institute Pastoral Development Network Paper No. 24f, London: ODI.

Hill, A.G. (1988), 'Population growth and rural transformation in tropical

References

Africa', in D. Rimmer (ed.): *Rural Transformation in Tropical Africa*, pp. 16-35, London: Belhaven Press.

Hjort af Ornas, A. (1990), 'Pastoral and environmental security in East Africa', *Disasters* 14/2: 115-22.

Hogg, R. (1980), 'Pastoralism and impoverishment: the case of the Isiolo Boran of Northern Kenya', *Disasters*, 6/3: 299-310.

Hogg, R. (1985), *Restocking Pastoralists in Kenya: A Strategy for Relief and Rehabilitation*, Overseas Development Institute Pastoral Development Network Paper 19c, London: ODI.

Hogg, R. (1986), 'The new pastoralism: poverty and dependency in Northern Kenya', *Africa* 56/3: 319-33.

Hogg, R. (1987), 'ODA Tsetse Transition Phase Project: Preliminary Socio-economic Baseline Survey and Monitoring Procedure for Middle Shabeele Tsetse Eradication Project', Interim Report (unpublished), London: ODA.

Hoksbergen, R. (1986), 'Approaches to the evaluation of development interventions: the importance of world and life views', *World Development* 14/2: 283-300.

Hopcraft, P.N. (1981), 'Economic institutions and pastoral resources management: considerations for a development strategy', in Galaty, Aronson, and Salzman (eds.) 1981, pp. 224-40.

le Houérou, H.N. (1977), 'The nature and causes of desertization', in M. H. Glantz (ed.): *Desertification: Environmental Degradation In and Around Arid Lands*, pp.17-38. Boulder: Westview Press.

Hudson, N.W. (1987), *Soil and Water Conservation in Semi-arid Areas*, FAO Soils Bulletin 57, Rome: FAO.

Hudson, N.W. (1992), *Land Husbandry*, London: Batsford.

Hyder, D.N. and **R.E. Bement** (1977), 'The status of grazing and rest in grazing management', in *The Impact of Herbivores on Arid and Semi-Arid Rangelands*, Proceedings of the Second United States/Australian Rangeland Panel, Perth: Australian Rangeland Society, pp.73-82.

IFAD (International Fund for Agricultural Development) (1986) *Soil and Water Conservation in Sub-Saharan Africa: Issues and Options*, Centre for Development Cooperation Services, University of Amsterdam.

IIED (International Institute for Environment and Development) (1991), *Pastoral Land Tenure in Africa: Programme for Research Support and Institutional Collaboration, London:* IIED.

ILCA (International Livestock Centre for Africa) (1979) 'Trypanotolerant livestock in West and Central Africa', *Monograph 2*, Addis Ababa: ILCA.

Iliffe, J. (1989), 'Review article: the origins of African population growth', *Journal of African History* 30: 165-9.

Joss, P.J., P.W. Lynch, and **O.B. Williams** (eds.) (1986), *Rangelands: a*

Resource Under Siege, Proceedings of the Seocnd International Rangeland Congress, Canberra: Australian Academy of Science.

Korten, D.C. (1980), 'Community organisation and rural development: a learning process approach', *Public Administration Review*, September/October 1980.

Kitching, G. (1983), 'Proto-industrialisation and demographic change', *Journal of African History* 24: 221-40.

Lane, C. and **J. Swift** (1989), *East African Pastoralism: Common Land, Common Problem*, Issues Paper No. 8, London: IIED.

Lappe, F.M., **J. Collins**, and **D. Kinley** (1981), *Aid as Obstacle: Twenty Questions About Our Foreign Aid and the Hungry*, San Francisco: Institute for Food and Development Policy.

Lodge, G.M., and **R.D.B. Whalley** (1985), 'The manipulation of species composition of natural pastures by grazing management', *Australian Rangeland Journal* 7: 6-16.

Low, A. (1980), *The Estimation and Interpretation of Pastoralists' Price Responsiveness*, Overseas Development Institute Pastoral Development Network Paper 10c, London: ODI.

McCabe, J.T. (1990), 'Success and failure: the breakdown of traditional drought coping institutions among the pastoral Turkana of Kenya', *Journal of Asian and African Studies* XXV: 3-4, 146-60.

McCarthy, J.W., **C. Clapp-Wincek**, **S. Londner**, and **A. Thomas** (1985), *A Soil and Water Conservation Project in Two Sites in Somalia: Seventeen Years Later*, Aid Project Impact Evaluation Report No. 62, Washington: United States Agency for International Development.

Meir, A. (1986), 'Demographic transition theory: a neglected aspect of the nomadism-sedentarism continuum', *Transactions of the Institute of British Geographers*, N.S.11, 199-211.

Moremi, T.C. (1990), 'Drought planning and response: Botswana experience', in D.A. Wilhite, W.E. Easterling, and D.A. Wood (eds.): *Planning for Drought: Toward a Reduction of Societal Vulnerability*, pp. 445-51, Boulder: Westview Press.

Moris, I.R. (1988), *Oxfam's Kenya Restocking Projects*, Overseas Development Institute Pastoral Development Network Paper 26c, London: ODI.

Morss, E.R. and **D.D. Gow** (eds.) (1985), *Implementing Rural Development Projects: Lessons from AID and the World Bank*, Boulder, Colorado: Westview Press.

Morss, E.R., **D.D. Gow**, and **C.W. Nordlinger** (1985), 'Sustaining project benefits', in Morss and Gow (eds.) 1985.

Morss, E.R. and **G.H. Honadle** (1985), 'Differing agendas' in Morss and Gow

References

(eds.) 1985, pp. 199-215.

Oakley, P. (1991), *Projects With People: The Practice of Participation in Rural Development*, Geneva: International Labour Office.

Oakley, P. and **D. Marsden** (1984), *Approaches to Participation in Rural Development*, Geneva: International Labour Office.

Oba, G. and **W. Lusigi** (1987), *An Overview of Drought Strategies and Land Use in African Pastoral Systems*, Overseas Development Institute Pastoral Development Network Paper 23a, London: ODI.

Odell, M.J. (1982), *Local Institutions and Management of Communal Resources: Lessons from Africa and Asia*, Overseas Development Institute Pastoral Development Network Paper 14e, London: ODI.

Oxby, C. (1982), *Group Ranches in Africa*, Overseas Development Institute Pastoral Development Network Paper 13d, London: ODI.

Oxby, C. (1985), *Settlement Schemes for Herders in the Subhumid Tropics of West Africa: Issues of Land Rights and Ethnicity*, Overseas Development Institute Pastoral Development Network Paper 19f, London: ODI.

Oxby, C. (1989), *African Livestock Keepers in Recurrent Crisis: Policy Issues Arising from the NGO Response*, London: IIED.

Pacey, A. and **A. Cullis** (1986), *Rainwater Harvesting: the Collection of Rainfall and Runoff in Rural Areas*, London: Intermediate Technology Publications.

Park, P. (1986), 'Social dimensions of harvesting rainwater in Turkana', *Waterlines* 5: 10-11.

Pratt, D.J. and **M.D. Gwynne** (eds.) (1977), *Rangeland Management and Ecology in East Africa*, London: Hodder and Stoughton.

Prior, J.C. (1992a), 'Planning for Pastoral Development in the Third World: Histories, the Erigavo Case Study, and Future Directions', thesis for Master's degree in Urban and Regional Planning, University of New England.

Prior, J.C. (1992b), 'Evaluating the experience of Third World soil and water conservation projects: nine common shortcomings' in *People Protecting Their Land*, Proceedings of the Seventh International Soil Conservation Organisation Conference, Sydney, September 1992, pp. 420-6, Sydney: ISCO.

Rapp, A. (1976), 'Introduction' in A. Rapp, H.N. Le Hou)rou and Lundholm (eds.): *Can Desert Encroachment Be Stopped?*, pp. 11-18, Ecological Bulletins/NFR 24, Stockholm: Swedish Natural Science Research Council.

Reij, C. (1987), 'The Agro-Forestry Project in Burkina Faso: an Analysis of Popular Participation in Soil and Water Conservation', unpublished paper presented to Oxfam Arid Lands Workshop, Cotonou, Benin, March 1987.

Reij, C. (1988), 'Soil and water conservation in sub-Saharan Africa: a bottom-up approach', *Appropriate Technology* 14/4: 14-16.

Reusse, E. (1982), 'Somalia's nomadic livestock economy', *World Animal*

Review 43: 2-9.

de Ridder, N. and **K.T. Wagenaar** (1986), 'A comparison between the productivity of traditional livestock systems and ranching in Eastern Botswana' in Joss, Lynch and Williams (eds.) 1986.

Rogers, D.J. and **S.E. Randolph** (1988), 'Tsetse flies in Africa: bane or boon?', *Conservation Biology* 2/1: 57-65.

Rondinelli, D.A. (1983), *Development Projects as Policy Experiments: an Adaptive Approach to Development Administration*, New York: Methuen.

Salih, M.S. (1978), 'Economics and problems of rangeland productivity in Sudan', *Proceedings of the First International Rangeland Congress*, Denver, Denver: Society for Range Management, pp. 134-6.

Salzman, P.C. (1980), *When Nomads Settle: Processes of Sedentarisation as Adaption and Response*, New York: Praeger.

Sandford, S. (1976), *Pastoral Human Populations*, Overseas Development Institute Pastoral Development Network Paper 2c, London: ODI.

Sandford, S. (1981) *Pastoralists as Animal Health Workers: The Range Development Project in Ethiopia*, Overseas Development Institute Pastoral Development Network Paper 12c, London: ODI.

Sandford, S. (1983), *Management of Pastoral Development in the Third World*, London: Wiley.

Sandford, S. (1985), *Better Livestock Policies for Africa*, ALPAN Network Paper 1, Addis Ababa: International Livestock Centre for Africa.

Schneider, H.K. (1981), 'Livestock as food and money' in Galaty, Aronson and Salzman (eds.) (1981), pp. 210-23.

Schneider, H.K. (1984), 'Livestock in African culture and society: a historical perspective' in Simpson and Evangelou (1984),. pp.187-99.

Selden, S.M. (1986), 'Put Mothers First: Maternal Mortality in a Remote Region of Somalia', Master of Public Health thesis, University of Sydney.

Seyoum, E. and **J. McIntire** (1986), 'A review of econometric supply response estimates for livestock products', Working Paper, ALPAN Supplement to Newsletter 4, Addis Ababa: ILCA.

Shepherd, G. (1988), *The Reality of the Commons: Answering Hardin from Somalia*, Overseas Development Institute Social Forestry Network Paper 6d, London: ODI.

Sikana, P.M. and **C.K. Kerven** (1991), *The Impact of Commercialisation on the Role of Labour in African Pastoral Societies*, Overseas Development Institute Pastoral Development Network Paper 31c, London: ODI.

Simpson, J.R. (1984), 'Problems and constraints, goals and policy: conflict resolution in development of sub-Saharan Africa's livestock industry' in Simpson and Evangelou 1984, pp. 5-20.

Simpson, J.R. and **P. Evangelou** (eds.) (1984), *Livestock Development in*

References

Subsaharan Africa: Constraints, Prospects, Policy, Boulder: Westview.

Skovlin, J.M. and **D.L. Williamson** (1978), 'Bush control and associated Tsetse fly problems of rangeland development on the coastal plain of East Africa', *Proceedings of the First International Rangeland Congress*, Denver, pp. 581-3, Denver: Society for Range Management.

Sollod, A.E., K. Wolfgang, and **J.A. Knight** (1984), 'Veterinary anthropology: interdisciplinary methods in pastoral systems research' in Simpson and Evangelou 1984, pp. 303-16.

Spencer, P. (1973), *Nomads in Alliance: Symbiosis and Growth Among the Rendille and Samburu of Kenya*, London: Oxford University Press.

Stiles, D. (1981), 'Relevance of the past in projections about pastoral peoples' in Galaty, Aronson and Salzman (eds.) 1981, pp.370-78.

Sullivan, G.M. (1984), 'Impact of government policies on the performance of the livestock-meat subsector' in Simpson and Evangelou 1984, pp.143-59.

Sutter, J.W. (1987), 'Cattle and inequality: herd size differences and pastoral production among the Fulani of Northeastern Senegal', *Africa* 57/2: 196-217.

Sweet, R.J. (1986), 'Grazing systems on degraded rangeland in Botswana' in Joss, Lynch and Williams (eds.) 1986, pp. 248-9.

Swift, J. (1976), 'The development of livestock trading in a nomadic pastoral economy: the Somali case' in *Pastoral Production and Society*, Proceedings of the International Meeting on Nomadic Pastoralism, Paris, December 1976, pp. 447-56, Cambridge: Cambridge University Press.

Swift, J. (1977), 'Pastoral development in Somalia: herding cooperatives as a strategy against desertification and famine' in M. H. Glantz (ed.): *Desertification: Environmental Degradation In and Around Arid Lands*, pp. 275-305, Boulder: Westview.

Swift, J. (1982), 'The future of African hunter-gatherer and pastoral peoples', *Development and Change* 13/2: 159-81.

Swift, J. and **A. Maliki** (1984), *A Cooperative Development Experiment Among Nomadic Herders in Niger*, Overseas Development Institute Pastoral Development Network Paper 18c, London: ODI.

Tendler, J. (1982), *Turning Private Voluntary Organisations into Development Agencies: Questions for Evaluation*, USAID Program Evaluation Discussion Paper No. 12, Washington: USAID.

Timberlake, L. (1985), *Africa in Crisis: the Causes, the Cures of Environmental Bankruptcy*, London: International Institute for Environment and Development.

Toulmin, C. (1986), *Pastoral Livestock Losses and Post-Drought Rehabilitation in Subsaharan Africa: Policy Options and Issues*, ALPAN Network Paper 8, Addis Ababa: International Livestock Centre for Africa.

Trail, J.C.M. and **K.E. Gregory** (1984), 'Animal breeding in Subsaharan

Africa: toward an integrated program for improving productivity' in Simpson and Evangelou (1984), pp. 107-21.

United Nations (1982), *Demographic Indicators of Countries: Estimates and Projections as Assessed in 1980*, New York: UN.

United States Agency for International Development (1972), *Desert Encroachment on Arable Lands: Significance, Causes and Control*, Washington: USAID.

United States Agency for International Development (1973), Implementation of New Directions in Development Assistance, Report for the US Congress, House Committee on International Relations, Washington: Government Printing Office.

United Nations Conference on Desertification (1977a), *Desertification Around the World*, United Nations document A/CONF. 74/2.

United Nations Conference on Desertification (1977b), *Desertification: Its Causes and Consequences*, Oxford: Pergamon Press.

United Nations Economic Commission for Africa (1985), *Comprehensive Policies and Programmes for Livestock Development in Africa: Problems, Constraints and Necessary Future Action*, African Livestock Policy Analysis Network Paper No.5, Addis Ababa.

Uphoff, N. (1990), 'Paraprojects as new modes of international development assistance', *World Development* 18/10: 1401-11.

Valentin, C. (1985), 'Effects of grazing and trampling on soil deterioration around recently drilled waterholes in the Sahelian zone' in S.A. El-Swaify, W.C. Moldenhauer and A. Lo (eds.): *Soil Erosion and Conservation*, pp. 51-65, Ankeny: Soil Conservation Society of America.

Weiner, M.L. (1984), 'The World Bank' in B.E. Cracknell (ed.): *The Evaluation of Aid Projects and Programmes* — Proceedings of a Conference organised by ODA and the Institute of Development Studies at the University of Sussex 7-8 April 1983, pp. 94-101, London: Overseas Development Administration.

Westoby, M., B. Walker, and **I. Noy-Meir** (1989), 'Opportunistic management for rangelands not at equilibrium', *Journal of Range Management* 42/4: 266-74.

White, C. (1984), *Herd Reconstruction: The Role of Credit Among Wodaabe Herders in Central Niger*, Overseas Development Institute Pastoral Development Network Paper 18d, London: ODI.

White, J.M. and **S.J. Meadows** (1981), 'Evaluation of the Contribution of Group and Individual Ranches in Kajiado District to Economic and Social Development', unpublished report.

Williams, O.B. (1974), 'Grazing management in the arid areas of Australia' in *The Impact of Herbivores on Arid and Semi-Arid Rangelands.* Proceedings of

References

the Second United States/Australia Rangeland Panel, Perth: Australian Rangeland Society, pp. 83-92.

Wilson, A.D. (1977), 'Grazing management in the arid areas of Australia' in *The Impact of Herbivores on Arid and Semi-Arid Rangelands*. Proceedings of the Second United States/Australia Rangeland Panel, Perth: Australian Rangeland Society, pp. 83-92.

Wilson, A.D., G.N. Harrington, and **I.F. Beale** (1984), 'Grazing management' in G.N. Harrington, A.D. Wilson and M.D. Young (eds.) 1984: *Management of Australia's Rangelands*, pp.129-39, Canberra: CSIRO.

Worby, E. (1988), 'Livestock policy and development ideology in Botswana' in D.W. Attwood, T.C. Bruneau and J.G. Galaty (eds.): *Power and Poverty: Development and Development Projects in the Third World*, pp.155-80, Boulder: Westview.

World Bank (1989a), *Sub-Saharan Africa: From Crisis to Sustainable Growth*, Washington: World Bank.

World Bank (1989b), *Successful Development in Africa: Case Studies of Projects, Programs, and Policies*, EDI Development Policy Case Series Analytical Case Studies No. 1, Washington: World Bank.

World Bank (1992), *World Development Report 1992*, New York: Oxford University Press.

Younger, S.D. and **E.G. Bonkoungou** (1989), 'Burkina Faso: the *Projet Agro-Forestier* — a case study of agricultural research and extension' in Economic Development Institute of the World Bank: *Successful Development in Africa: Case Studies of Projects, Programs, and Policies*, pp. 11-26, Washington: World Bank.

Zeissan, K.H. (1986), 'First livestock and disease data for Central Somalia: outlook and recommendations' in R.G. Wieland (ed.): *Future Range/Livestock Development Strategies for the Central Rangelands of Somalia*, Proceedings of the seminar and workshop held in Mogadishu, Somalia, March 1986, pp. 67-76, Mogadishu: Central Rangelands Development Project.

Index

Acacia 58
ACCOMPLISH NGO (Sudan) 39
adaptive change 121, 127, 129
adverse policy environments 50-1
advocacy role of NGOs 128
agricultural land 62-3
aid agencies
   development style 52, 71-2, 80-1, 92
   intervention as political entity 88
   predomination of goals of agency 51-4
alternative employment programmes 125
Australian International Development Assistance Bureau (AIDAB) 53
autonomous replicate model 112-19
   evolution and devolution of frame work 118-19
   feedback and interaction 116
   policy executive 114, 115
   proposed initial organisational frame work 114-18

banking 67
beel 80, 81
beneficiaries
   disaster intervention planning 40
   exclusion from planning stage 38-43
   maintenance by 30, 31, 38
   organisational skills 44
   participation evaluation 92-3
   participation monitoring 91
   participatory development 42
berkets 98
boreholes 45-6
Botswana 40

bovine theileriosis 39

cash economy 66, 68
Central Rangelands Development Project (CRDP) 45, 47
cereal banks 109, 124
clan structure and conflict 80
climate 4
'climax community' succession 17
commercialisation of livestock production 13, 14-16, 27-9, 68
   exports 14, 61, 66
   impact of 15-16
communities
   autonomous replicate model, in 118-19
   credibility with 73, 87-8, 98-100
   elders 85-6, 91, 105
   group cooperation 81
   institution building 43-4
   inter-community decision making 98-9
   inter-community relations 106-7
   organisational skills 84, 90, 94
   Oxfam development style 71-2
   participation *see* community participation
   reducing vulnerability of 122-4
   women 82, 87, 91
   young men 85-6, 87-8, 91
   see also beneficiaries; kinship ties
community development 43-4
   development style 106-8
   Erigavo project 82-4
   keeper of tools 83, 85, 93
   monitoring 91

Index

Oxfam and 80-1
politics and 84-95
strategies 82-4
trainee choice 83, 93
community participation 88
evaluation 92-3
monitoring 91
contagious bovine pleuro pneumonia 39
credit schemes 109, 122

data collection *see* information collection
debt burdens 124
decision making
economic stratification and 67-8
factors influencing 4
group frameworks 99
inter-community 98-9
political relationships 99-100
poor understanding of process 30-2
public meetings 91
desertification 16
design of projects
data collection 35-6
faults attributable to poor design 44-9
flexibility 35
human factor importance 37-8
inherent failures 35-8
justice as goal 48-9
process approach 36
learning process 72-6, 110
project approach 36
sustainability as goal 48-9
wrong technology 45-8
development
ideologies 51-4
meaning 4
agency or beneficiaries 76, 78-82
Oxfam's 78, 80
model *see* development model
participatory *see* participatory development
policy *see* development policy
projects *see* design of projects; development projects; failure of development projects
style 52, 71-2, 80-1, 92
development model
autonomous replicate *see* autonomous replicate model

expanding NGO model 112
flexibility 110
identification of 109-19
sustainability 111
theoretical requirements 110-11
development policy
access to water 125
adaptive change 121, 127, 129
alternative employment 125
education 125-6
health services 125-6
land degradation causes and 126-7
mobility 125
new directions 121-8
reducing vulnerability of communities 122-4
security improvements 126
development projects
desired results 23-4
failure *see* failure of development projects
history 23-55
small scale 95, 105-6, 107-8, 110
development style 52, 71-2
community development model 80-1
evaluation of 92
'dia-paying' groups 80, 81
disaster intervention 40
disaster mitigation 24, 121
disaster seen as inevitable 122
kinship ties 40
post-drought recovery mechanisms 40, 41-2, 109
predisposing factors 122
reducing vulnerability of communities 122-4
risk-spreading 40
transhumance 40
drought
coping with 40
post-drought recovery and restocking 40, 41-2, 109
susceptibility to 102, 121

East Coast fever 39-40
education 125-6
employment, alternative 125
eradication of tsetse fly 25, 26, 45
overgrazing after 26

Erigavo project
  defining problem 56-70
  development style 71-2
  strengths and limitations 106-8
  erosion control
    community development strategies 82-4
    community participation 88, 91, 92-3
    credibility establishment 87-8
    definition of development 76, 78-82
    evaluation of activities 91-5
    impact evaluation 94-5
    monitoring 90-1
    political instrument, as 84-95
    sustainability 93-4
    trainees 83, 93
    training 76, 78
    visible benefits 73
  information collection 72-6
  personnel 117
  rangeland management 97-108
    access to water 99-100
    credibility building 98-100
    evaluation 104-6
    grazing reserves 102-3
    potential solutions 102-4
    problem definition 101-2
    reversion of privatisation 102-4
  social causes of degradation 58-61
  social framework 80-1
  Women's Development Officer 82
Erigavo range privatisation 58-60, 61-3
erosion control *see* Erigavo project, erosion control; land degradation; soil and water conservation (SWC) projects
evaluation
  community participation 92-3
  development style 92
  Erigavo project
    erosion control 91-5
    rangeland management 104-6
  ex post project evaluation 49, 91
  flexibility 92
  impacts 94-5
  sustainability 93-4
ex post project evaluation 49, 91
expanding NGO model 112
experts 4-5

failure of development projects
  aid agency goals predominating 51-4
  beneficiaries excluded from planning stage 38-43
  data base poor 25-30
  decision-making processes, poor understanding of 30-2
  external factors 24, 49-54
  generalisations about planning 32-4
  government failure to support 43-4
  government hostility 50-1
  institution building, neglect of 43-4
  internal factors 24, 25-49
  omission of goals of justice 48-9
  personnel lack of planning skills 37-8
  planning failures 35-44
  poor design *see* design of projects
  problem definition inadequate 25-30
  'top-down' design 35-8
famine
  interventions 9
  predisposing factors 122
  see also disaster mitigation
Famine Early Warning Systems (FEWS) 40, 122
fertility rates 9
flexibility 72, 110
  financial 92
  lack of 35
  technical 92
food production 122
food security 40
food storage 124

Ghana market-control interventions 28
Gir Gir Group Ranch, Kenya 11, 41
governments
  failure to support projects 43-4
  hostility to projects 50-1
  indigenous 43
  institution building 43-4
  preference for large projects 106
  range privatisation and 104
  small-scale projects and 105-6
grain banks 109, 124
grazing controls 25, 29, 30
  failure to involve beneficiaries 39
grazing reserves 45, 102-3
GTZ (German bilateral agency) 47

Index

health services 125-6
Hol Hol well 99-100
house construction 59-60

impact evaluation 94-5
indigenous institutions 111
indigenous technical knowledge 43
information collection
  bias of observer 75, 76
  Erigavo project 72-6
  individual interviews 74, 75
  informal group discussions 74-5
  participant observation 74, 75-6
  poor 25-30
  population data 7
  structured group discussions 74
  throughout project 35-6
  unstated processes 75-6
inter-community decision making 98-9
inter-community relations 106-7
interventions
  community level 71
  famine relief 9, 40
  low cost 72
  market interventions 27-8
  see also development projects

justice
  goals of 48-9
  NGOs and 106

keeper of tools
  choice of 83, 85, 93
Kenya
  Gir Gir Group Ranch 11, 41
  post-drought restocking 41-2
  Tarbaj 36
kinship ties 100
  group cooperation 80, 81
  maintenance need 31
  risk-spreading 40
  weakening 13, 65, 121

land degradation 16-21, 121
  borehole drilling 45-6
  declining trend 17
  desertification 16
  development policy, in 126-7
  ecosystem stability preservation 17
  meaning 17
  over-grazing 16, 26
  pastoralist population increase and 7-8
  primary causes 20, 21
  settlement and 58, 101
  social causes 58-61
  soil loss 17, 20, 30, 101
  stabilisation of gullies 83
  'Tragedy of the Commons' thesis 16, 34
  vegetation loss 16, 17, 30, 58, 101
  see also Erigavo project, erosion control; soil and water conservation (SWC) projects
land privatisation *see* privatisation of range
land tenure 101, 124-5
  traditional systems 58
  see also privatisation of range
learning process approach 72-6, 110
livestock
  commercialisation of production 13, 14-16, 27-9, 61, 66, 68
  exports 14, 61, 66
  impact of 15-16
  maximisation of numbers, reasons for 33
  multiple values attributed to 32
  post-drought restocking 40, 41-2, 109
  range enclosure effects 13-14
  stock reduction schemes 32
  subsistence production 14
  traditional production 122
  water-point development 25, 30-1
local social framework 80-1
low-cost interventions 72
low-cost technologies 44

market economy 107
market interventions 27-8
mobility loss *see* sedentarisation
monitoring
  Erigavo project 90-1

negotiations 88, 110, 119
nomads 2, 3, 60-1
non-governmental organisations (NGOs) 4
  advocacy role 128
  autonomous replicate model 112-19

147

comparative advantage 110
development ideologies 53-4
expanding NGO model 112
indigenous 111
local 118-19

over-grazing 16, 26
Oxfam
  community development model 80-1
  development style 71-2
  small-scale projects 107-8

paraveterinary programmes 39-40, 47, 109
participant observation 74, 75-6
participatory development 42, 92
  community participation 88, 91
  disadvantages 42-3
  indigenous technical knowledge 43
  meaning of participation 42
  see also beneficiaries
pastoral development projects see development projects
pastoral environment
  generalisations 32-4
  interactive nature 25
  meaning 3-4
  pastoralists see pastoralists
  political economic changes 13
  population see population
pastoralists
  agro-pastoralists 3
  alternative employment programmes 125
  decision making 4, 30-2, 67-8, 91, 98-100
  definition 2-3
  economic stratification 67-8
  land available to 10
  mobility 31, 125
  mobility loss see sedentarisation
  nomadic 2, 3
  population see population
  preoccupation with 'mainstream' notions about 33-4
  sedentarisation see sedentarisation
  sedentary 2, 3, 59
  semi-nomadic 2, 3, 19, 59
  transhumance see semi-nomadic
personnel

Erigavo project 117
lack of planning skills 37-8
political conflicts 120-1
political processes and development 56-7
politics
  community development strategy and 84-95
population
  data quality 7
  demographic transition argument 8, 9
  density 8, 10-12, 121
  fertility rates 9
  growth rates 6-7, 9, 11
  increases 6-9
  land degradation and 7-8
post-drought recovery and restocking 40, 41-2, 109
price controls 27-8
privatisation of range 12, 58-9
  disputes 62, 63
  economic costs and benefits 66-8
  Erigavo 58-60, 61-3
  land degradation and 101
  nomadic herding movements and 60-1
  reclassification as agricultural land 62-3
  reversion process 102-4
  social costs and benefits 63-5
problem definition 120-1
  by pastoralists 101-2
  inadequate 25-30
  political component 120
process approach to design 36
  learning process 72-6, 110
projects see design of projects; development projects; failure of development projects

rainfall 4
ranch co-operatives 62
ranching schemes 25, 26-7, 31, 39, 45
range
  communal ownership 14
  degradation see land degradation
  ecosystem 18
  enclosure 13-14
  privatisation 12, 58-61
  disputes 62, 63
  economic costs and benefits 66-8
  Erigavo 58-60, 61-3

Index

land degradation and 101
nomadic herding movements and 60-1
reversion process 102-4
social costs and benefits 63-5
reclassification as agricultural land 62-3
see also Erigavo project, rangeland management
range management
Erigavo see Erigavo project, rangeland management
long benefit-return periods 98
relationship-building 99
restocking 40, 41-2, 109
rinderpest 39
risk-spreading 40

sedentarisation 121
as development issue 126
conflicts over water 46
land degradation and 101
pastoral communities 12-14
prerequisites for settlement 12-13
process 58-61
spontaneous 12
settlement see sedentarisation
small-scale projects 95, 107-8, 110
independence from government 105-6
social framework 80-1
traditional 13
see also kinship ties
soil and water conservation (SWC) projects 109
behaviour modification 30-1
maintenance 38
technologies 78, 79
visible benefits 98
soil loss 17, 20, 30, 101
see also Erigavo project, erosion control; land degradation; soil and water conservation (SWC) projects
Somali civil war 46, 91, 104, 110
Somalia
borehole drilling 45-6
Central Rangelands Development Project (CRDP) 45, 47
control of water 31
eradication of tsetse fly 26
paravets in 47
see also Erigavo project

stock reduction schemes 32
storage facilities 124
structure maintenance 30, 31, 38
subsistence livestock production 14
sustainability 71, 111
evaluation of 93-4
goal of project 48-9
Swaziland market interventions 27

Tanzania market-control interventions 28
Tarbaj (Kenya) 36
technicians 48
technologies
complexity 47
ignorance of past mistakes 48
inappropriate 78, 79
low-cost 44
poor management 47
wrong 45-8
tick-borne diseases 47
tools 94
keeper of tools 83, 85, 93
loan of 84
retrieval of 87
trucks 94
'Tragedy of the Commons' thesis 16, 34
trainees, choice of 83, 93
training 76, 78
information collection during 75
technicians 48
tribalism 75, 80, 110
inter-tribal consensus 116
Tsetse fly eradication 25, 26, 45

vaccines, veterinary 40
vegetation
climax community succession 17
grazing controls 25, 29, 30, 39, 45, 102-3
irreversible trend 19
loss 16, 17, 30, 58, 101
perennial pasture species loss 101
rangeland ecosystem 18
veterinary schemes
bovine theileriosis 39
contagious bovine pleuro pneumonia 39
East Coast fever 39-40
paravets 39-40, 47, 109
rinderpest 39

149

tick-borne diseases 47

water
   access to 99-100, 125
   inappropriate technologies 45
   livestock water-point development 25, 30-1
   source of conflict 46
well construction 98
   inappropriate technologies 45
   land degradation and 45-6
wells
   Hol Hol well 99-100
   livestock watering 25
   seizure and control 46
women   63-5, 66-7, 68, 72, 74-5, 82, 86, 87, 91, 98
Women's Development Officer 82

www.ingramcontent.com/pod-product-compliance
Lightning Source LLC
Chambersburg PA
CBHW050553300426
44112CB00013B/1903